Kingdom concerns

Kingdom concerns

A biblical theology of mission today

Ken Gnanakan

Inter-Varsity Press

INTER-VARSITY PRESS
38 De Montfort Street, Leicester LE1 7GP, UK

© 1989, 1993 by Theological Book Trust

First published 1989 by Theological Book Trust, PO Box 3408, Bangalore 560 034, India. This edition first published by Inter-Varsity Press, Leicester, UK, in 1993.

British Library Cataloguing-in-Publication Data
A catalogue record for this book is available from the British Library.

ISBN 0-85110-698-6

Set in Linotron Palatino

Photoset by Parker Typesetting Service, Leicester

Printed in Great Britain
by Cox & Wyman Ltd, Reading, Berkshire

Inter-Varsity Press is the book-publishing division of the Universities and Colleges Christian Fellowship (formerly the Inter-Varsity Fellowship), a student movement linking Christian Unions in universities and colleges throughout the United Kingdom and the Republic of Ireland, and a member movement of the International Fellowship of Evangelical Students. For information about local and national activities write to UCCF, 38 De Montfort Street, Leicester LE1 7GP.

Contents

Foreword

It is a privilege for me to write this Foreword. I have known Ken Gnanakan from his early Christian days as a musician and evangelist with Youth for Christ, through his development as a preacher and teacher of God's Word, and in recent years as a theologian and missiologist.

Reading *Kingdom Concerns* has been a very absorbing experience. The treatment is both simple and profound. Ken Gnanakan handles the vital themes of today's debates with the ease of an erudite scholar who is in touch with both the world and the church.

Gnanakan's handling of mission issues debated by ecumenicals and evangelicals is to be appreciated. He deals with topics such as the God–world–church sequence, humanization, dialogue and justice, with assurance and with strong scriptural background. He also deals with issues raised by liberation theologians and eco-theologians. In fact, he has not left out any topic that is currently debated in discussions on missions.

There is much talk about justice from all sections of the church, and some stray far from the biblical understanding of this vital theme. We need to take note of Ken Gnanakan's statement, 'The prophets' cry for justice came in the context of a theocratic people.' It is true that 'the primary thrust of mission . . . is to present the God of justice rather than to emphasize the justice of God' (p. 93).

Ken Gnanakan also points out various issues in which evangelical missiologists tend to go overboard, such as numerical church growth, success and an overemphasis on 'goal-setting and strategizing for mission programmes with neat and carefully worked out plans'. He points out that the claim of some to have achieved the pattern of New

9

Testament churches is a fallacy. These are timely cautions to be taken note of by those who are involved in missions.

Mission needs to be related to our particular contexts. So much missiology is directly transferred from the West to our situations without the necessary sensitivity. Ken Gnanakan's treatment deals with subjects such as suffering, the role of the Holy Spirit and the attributes of God as a holy and angry God. These topics are very relevant to our Asian context and have not been emphasized in mission theology as they should be.

Having read through *Kingdom Concerns* and appreciated it very much, I recommend this book as a textbook on the theology of missions for our missionary training centres in Asia and around the world. As we develop missionary training centres in two-thirds-world missions, this book meets a great need. At a time when we need more evangelical theological books written in Asia, Ken Gnanakan's contribution is very welcome.

Theodore Williams
Indian Evangelical Mission,
World Evangelical Fellowship

Preface

My real involvement in theology began with my theologizing for the Indian context in 1979 with the implement-
ation of the ACTS Institute – a vision the Lord had given me
during my studies in London. The vision was timely. Not
only did it challenge my wholly academic involvement in
theology; it brought me into a practical situation where I
was able to understand and work towards God's total
mission. I continue to marvel at the fact of God's gracious
dealings with humanity.

Throughout the growth of the ministry of the ACTS
Institute, and the opportunity to teach at the South Asia
Institute of Advanced Christian Studies, I have sensed deeply
the hand of God in the theology he was calling me to develop.
The result is *Kingdom Concerns*. This book began not just as a
writing project involving time and academic work, but as an
outflow of years of experience of learning and ministering.

One of my prime concerns has been to develop a 'biblical
theology'. I was involved in the sixth Asia Theological
Association Consultation in Seoul in 1982, and, in particular, in drafting the Declaration. I remember the intense
debate on the need for a theology that would be true both to
the Bible and to our context. We had stated:

> To be faithful to the Word of God and to be relevant
> to our cultures, all theological reflection should be
> patterned on 'the Word made flesh' . . . [to] enable
> the Bible to speak relevantly to its context.[1]

I had no doubt about the need to make our theology alive
and dynamic and to see it actually work in our everyday life.

11

But my own struggle was with the overemphasis on 'contextualization'. Its presuppositions and outworkings so seemed to focus on human effort that I came away with a deep desire to search the Scriptures for the kind of theology that would allow God himself to work out his purposes through his people. Yet this theology would have to take seriously both the Bible and our context. My own way of describing the integration of the two is in the word 'actualization'. It may not be the fullest way of expressing all that theology ought to be, but it makes the 'Word made flesh' idea central to the whole process of theologizing.

Writing *Kingdom Concerns* has been exciting. As I have studied the Bible afresh from the perspective of mission and constantly related it to the ministry God has given me, I have tried to articulate a theology which I am convinced should be central to our mission. My prayer is that this attempt at an 'actualized theology' will inspire others to write theology from their own missiological perspectives. It is this form of theologizing that will add richness to the church all over the world. I dedicate this book to all who seek to theologize for God's mission in the world today.

I first wrote this book for Asian readers, but have been repeatedly made aware of the need of such material all over the world. I am grateful to IVP for their willingness to make this book available more widely. Having this larger readership in mind, and having had some time to think through these insights, I have been able to make some revisions. The changes do not, however, represent any major shift from my earlier position.

I am grateful to God for giving me the privilege of being involved in his mission. I could have remained a cold academic had it not been for his gracious intervention and the challenge to set up the ACTS Institute. My theologizing is essentially an expression of my gratitude to God for the gift of his salvation.

Ken Gnanakan

PART 1

The historical setting of modern mission

1

From Edinburgh to Bangkok

In what was referred to as the 'flood-time of missionary optimism'[1] and characterized by a fervent evangelistic zeal, the World Missionary Conference at Edinburgh in 1910 marked a significant milestone in the history of missions. Its dynamic Chairman, the American Methodist Dr John R. Mott, exemplifying the optimism of the age, summed it up in his concluding address: 'The end of the conference is the beginning of the conquest.'[2] In many ways, this was the climax of the missionary zeal that had marked the nineteenth century.

William Carey's *An Enquiry into the Obligations of Christians, to use Means for the Conversion of the Heathens* had earlier made an impact with missionaries responding to the call to reach the world. He had argued that the Great Commission was still binding on Christians, and had exhorted the church in his day:

> As our blessed Lord has required us to pray that his kingdom may come, and his will be done on earth as it is in heaven, it becomes us not only to express our desires of that even by word, but to use every lawful method to spread the knowledge of his name.[3]

William Carey himself had dreamt of a World Missionary Conference to be held in the Cape of Good Hope in 1810.

At Edinburgh, there was little debate about the meaning of mission. The various commissions reported on carrying the gospel to all the non-Christian world, and reports were presented on such topics as the church of the mission field, education in relation to the Christianization of national life, and the missionary message in relation to non-Christian religions. The primary purpose of mission, however, was understood as the evangelization of the non-Christian world.

John Mott was the driving force of the conference. The memorable slogan which he had coined and propagated was heard far and wide: 'the evangelization of the world in this generation'. Several decades later, that challenge continued to confront Christians all over the world. The challenge was received, and young and old responded, knowing that the call to proclaim the gospel was imperative.

The International Missionary Council

The World Missionary Conference gave birth to a continuation committee with Mott as Chairman. A series of conferences followed in India, Burma, Singapore, China, Korea, Japan and other countries in 1912 and 1913. At a 1912 conference of South Indian missionaries including Mott, it was recorded that 'the conference realizes that there is a loud call for more direct preaching of the gospel all through the land and urges the importance of missions uniting for this purpose'.[4] It is hard to imagine what would have happened if the tempo had been allowed to build up unhindered. But then came the First World War. Not until 1918 was an emergency committee set up. This gradually formed the International Missionary Council (IMC), the first cooperative effort of its kind amongst Protestant missionary bodies.

The functions of the IMC were:

to stimulate thinking and investigation on missionary questions;

to help to coordinate the activities of the national missionary organizations in the different countries;

through common consultation to help to unite Christian public opinion in support of freedom of conscience and religion and of missionary liberty;

to help to unite the Christian forces of the world in seeking justice in international and intersocial relations, especially where politically weaker people are involved;

to be responsible for the publication of the *International Review of Missions* and such other publications as in the judgment of the committee may contribute to the study of missionary questions;

to call another world missionary conference if and when this should be desirable.

As one reads reports of those early conferences and of those held subsequently, it is hard to believe that the optimism and enthusiasm for evangelism with which IMC came into existence were so soon submerged by the concerns that have hampered and even opposed evangelistic effort. It is clear that Edinburgh 1910 and the IMC represented the climate that prevailed in the heyday of colonialism, when the 'missionary' spirit seemed to blend with the success of the colonizers. The German missionary thinker, Gustav Warneck, had attacked Mott's dream as symptomatic of the American dream of the conversion of the whole world within the span of a single generation. After two world wars, the rise of nationalism and the resurgence of non-Christian religions, the dream was soon to fade, and optimism had to be subdued by the kinds of attitudes more in keeping with the age.

Undoubtedly, there was a direct link between the success of colonial powers and the optimism of missionary movements. Colonialization and Christianization were seen to be synonymous, and some churches were only just beginning to fight for their independence. In fact, at the

Edinburgh Conference itself, V. S. Azariah, one of only two non-westerners to give major addresses, had hinted on the problems of cooperation between 'foreign and native workers'.[5] He gently rebuked the nature of the personal and official relationships that existed between the missionaries and the nationals.

> As long as this relationship exists, we must admit that no sense of self-respect and individuality can grow in the Indian church . . . There can never be real progress unless the aspirations of the native Christians to self-government and independence are accepted, encouraged and acted upon.[6]

The image of missionaries exploiting the powers of the colonial rule was widespread and had taken various forms. For instance, Mahatma Gandhi said:

> Unfortunately, Christianity in India has been inextricably mixed up for the last one hundred and fifty years with the British rule. It appears to us synonymous with materialistic civilization and imperialistic exploitation by the stronger races of the weaker races of the world.[7]

In the face of this and other criticisms, it is hardly surprising that the end of the colonial era brought about changes in the missionary movement. The optimism had to give way to realism, and crucial questions about the task of missions were soon to be asked.

Attitudes to non-Christian religions

It seems hard to believe that the body that endorsed evangelism was soon to question, even resist, it. At its conference in Jerusalem in 1928 the IMC appeared to begin to define the missionary task in relation to the newer challenges of that day. In place of the optimism of Edinburgh, an uncertainty about the task was evident. To be fair, there was apparently no shift of belief that the nature of the task was to proclaim Jesus Christ, for

> the Gospel is the answer to the world's greatest need. It is not our discovery or achievement, it rests on what we recognize as the act of God. It is first and foremost Good News. It announces Truth. Its very nature forbids us to say that it may be the right belief for some but not for others. Either it is true for all, or it is not true at all.[8]

Secularistic forces were soon challenging all religions. Fresh lines of communication were opened with people of other religions in an effort to counteract the opposition together. This resulted in uncertainty about the relationship of the Christian message to non-Christian religious and secular philosophies. The concepts of salvation, evangelism and conversion took on a meaning more acceptable to the non-Christian, and little attention was paid to doctrines such as the sinful nature of humanity, reconciliation, and redemption. An independent inquiry chaired by William Hocking, issued from Jerusalem in 1930, dealt with some of the crucial questions that were being asked.

For instance, the Hocking commission called for a positive attitude towards non-Christian religions, claiming that there was little reason for the Christian to believe that 'sincere and aspiring seekers after God in other religions are to be damned'.[9] There was a 'nucleus of religious truth' in all the creeds. The Hindu, the Muslim and the Buddhist had a religious intuition, and 'the God of this intuition is the true God'.[10]

This approach to other religions had obvious implications for beliefs about conversion, evangelism and proclamation. The attempt to convert Asia to 'Christian membership' was considered improper, and the missionaries, as foreigners, had in fact no right to seek the conversion of Asians to Christianity.

> It is clearly not the duty of the Christian missionary to attack the non-Christian systems of religion. Nor is it his primary duty to denounce the errors and abuses he sees in them . . . the Christian should realize that in his criticism he is joining Hindus in rectifying abuses which have invaded the structure of their religion . . . The Hindu can do far more toward any such reform than can he, the Christian, as an outsider.[11]

The Hocking inquiry reflected two moods. The first had to do with the change of attitude towards Christianity within the West itself. For instance, Ernst Troeltsch's famous book of 1901, *The Absoluteness of Christianity*, had reflected the earlier attitude and used terms such as 'final', 'unique' and 'normative'. In a lecture delivered in 1923, however, Troeltsch attacked his own earlier position, arguing that although Christianity was 'absolute' for Christians, other faiths were 'absolute' for their adherents.[12] This 'relative absoluteness' was now to be the Christian's attitude.

Another mood was reflected in Hocking's report. From the mission field came an attack on the conversionist mentality of the missionary. This had resulted in the Hindu Reform Movement, which, while opposing Christian conversion, sought to make Hinduism a more humane religion. Raja Ram Mohan Roy and others had sought to integrate some acceptable aspects of the Christian message into their own faith to give to it greater social impact. In keeping with such demands Hocking's report stated that 'a Christian will therefore regard himself a co-worker with the forces which are making for righteousness within every religious system'.[13] Christian missionaries, rather than seeking conversions, were to work in partnership with Hindus for the betterment of both religions and for common social reform.

The question arises: in what way is Christianity unique? The Hocking Report's approach was interesting: 'Christianity has many doctrines in common with other religions, yet no other religion has the same group of doctrines'.[14] If one thinks of uniqueness as a total contrast to other religions, Christianity is not unique. It is unique only in the way it brings together various beliefs also found in other religions. It is their particular juxtaposition in Christianity that is said to be distinctive.

Traditional evangelism, which had been the heartbeat of the missionary movement, could certainly find no room for such attitudes. The further question arises: is there any need to continue with missionary activity? Even if the answer is yes, what was to be the role of that activity? According to Hocking, ministry and service to human needs were to be the primary concern. Involvement in people's secular needs through educational and philanthropic mission work was, in fact, to be conducted in such a way that it would be 'free from responsibility to evangelization'.[15]

Despite the negative position of the Hocking report the issues raised have helped us take a more positive attitude to our social involvement. We must ask ourselves whether the desire to win 'converts' or even to plant churches should be our only motive for getting involved in God's world. The report claimed: 'We do agricultural missionary work because we are Christians, not because we want to make Christians.'[16] Rather than seeing this as an attack on evangelism, should we not learn from it? Perhaps our social action with its evangelistic motive is not biblically founded.

Tambaram 1938

The reactions to all this were severe, and at its next meeting in Tambaram, Madras, in 1938, the IMC had to focus its attention on the relationship of the Christian message to the messages of the non-Christian world. India was certainly an ideal location for this particular theme. Voices such as that of Mahatma Gandhi were still echoing, particularly since Mott himself had discussed the issue of conversion with him. Gandhi had said:

> I disbelieve in the conversion of one person by another. My effort should never be to undermine one's faith, but to make him a better follower of his faith. This implies belief in the truth of all religions and, therefore, respect for them. It again implies true humanity, a recognition of the fact that as the Divine Light has been vouchsafed to all religions through an imperfect medium of flesh, they must share, in more or less degree, the imperfection of the vehicle.[17]

Even before Edinburgh 1910, the West had been forcefully reminded of the claims of the world's ancient religions. The 1893 World Parliament of Religions in Chicago had heard the powerful oratory of Swami Vivekananda, who spoke of the continuing influence of Hinduism, along with his 'passion to push India forward'.[18] His stay in the USA for over a year after the conference was memorable. 'Wherever he went, he created a minor sensation not only by his presence but by what he said and how he said it. Having seen this Hindu Sanyasin once it was difficult to forget him or his message. In America he was called the "cyclonic Hindu".'[19] Vivekananda was unimpressed by the kind of Christianity he had seen, and, as a result, his faith in the Hindu philosophy became all the firmer. The American press, carried away by his charisma, criticized the churches for sending missionaries to the East when there was so much for westerners to learn from the Asians. Christianity had nothing unique to offer the East.

With all the pressures building up, Tambaram's task was difficult. But it seemed to be handled decisively. Largely influenced by the clear convictions of the missionary theologian Hendrik Kraemer, it reaffirmed the historic distinctiveness of the Christian revelation and a commitment to the 'unfinished evangelistic task of the church'.[20] Further, evangelism was clearly defined.

> By evangelism we understand that the church universal in all its branches and through the service of all its members, must so present Christ Jesus to the world in the power of the Holy Spirit that men shall come to put their trust in God through him, accept him as their Saviour and serve him as their Lord in the fellowship of his church.[21]

It was even made clear that

> evangelism is not due merely to the zeal of Christian people but rather the outcome of a divine initiative . . . But the task can never be achieved without sacrifice. Churches as well as individuals are summoned to die to themselves and to their own particular interests that the world may be saved. Worship must lead to witness and spiritual growth to self-giving.[22]

The task reaffirmed

When they summed up their task it seemed even clearer that the delegates were serious about making an impact on the secular and religious worlds in the West as well as in the East. Among the 800 million people of Europe and the American continent, 240 million people still claimed no connection with organized Christianity. In the so-called non-Christian countries, some, such as Afghanistan, the Soviet Republics, Bhutan, outer Mongolia, Nepal and Tibet, were closed to Christian witness. In China, where an enormous amount of resources and personnel had already been invested, 45% still remained untouched. In India, in addition to a large number of Indian states in which no missionaries reside, there are areas consisting of two, three and in one case five million people without effective Christian witness. The fact that there are only 14 Protestant missions and 700 Christians to a million people shows the magnitude of the unfinished task. The existence of 60 million of the depressed classes and aboriginal people is a call for continued effort. The evangelistic effort among the 80 million Muslims and Sikhs is at present wholly inadequate.[23]

Tambaram further attempted to spell out the place of the church in relation to this task, affirming that 'world evangelism is the God-given task of the church.'[24] The concept was of the church itself as the missionary to the world. Further, Tambaram emphasized that

the church's message to the world is the Lord Jesus Christ himself in all his manifold grace and power. It is the work of evangelism both to set forth the facts of his life upon earth and his teaching about God and man, and also to exalt and proclaim him, crucified, risen and glorified, that men may awaken to God and to a sense of their sin and separation from God, may be led to true repentance and to that act of will whereby they believe in and receive the forgiveness of their sins through Christ, and enter upon a new life to trust and obedience toward God and of abounding hope for this world and that which is to come.[25]

Rightly, the ministry of evangelism was firmly anchored within the church, and efforts were made to emphasize the evangelistic purpose of the whole range of the church's activities. The role of the church in the 'realization of such ends as justice, freedom and peace' were, however, also spelt out.[26] The Council declared that 'a living church cannot dissociate itself from prophetic and practical activities in regard to social conditions'.[27] Active service of the community is the inescapable consequence of the gospel. Care was taken to point out, however, that since 'social programmes grow out of the gospel, no one such programme can claim to be the content of the Christian message'.[28]

In discussing medical ministry, for instance, Tambaram stated that 'evangelism is implicit in all Christian medical work, but it calls for a definite expression by the medical staff through the spoken word'.[29] Further, Tambaram advocated a correlation between religious educational programmes and evangelism. 'Evangelism must be educational and education must be evangelistic.'[30] While this certainly presented a strong reply to the Hocking report, a fresh look at the Bible will reveal the shortcomings of this approach. Although some of the implications of Tambaram are valid, we must not allow the idea of *correlation* between social service and evangelism to lead to a *confusion* of the two.

For evangelicals, there appears to be little room for disagreement about this. But wider interpretations were introduced which led to a greater social emphasis later. 'The gospel of Christ carries with it the vision and hope of social transformation and of the realization of such ends as justice, freedom and peace.'[31] In the light of the broadening of evangelical concerns today, Tambaram can be seen as a distinctive landmark in its handling of the relationship of evangelism and its social implications.

As expected, the emphasis on the role of the church in changing the social and economic order of the world led to confusion.[32] As the old order breaks down, the Christian looks for nothing less than God's order, the kingdom of God. The Council was careful enough to point out that 'the kingdom of God is within history and yet it is beyond history.'[33] On the one hand, the kingdom is not to be identified with any present system or order. On the other, we are reminded that we can fall into the error of placing the kingdom of God beyond history. 'The kingdom is an eternal kingdom, but it is God's purpose that it should come within time and within this world.'[34] Further, to say that if we change individuals we will of necessity change the social order is only half the truth. Likewise, to say that social change will necessarily produce individual change is also only half the truth.

It was probably at this point that the dangers inherent in the enlarged understanding of the evangelistic task began to arise. While affirming the need for change, Tambaram attempted a definition of sin which included guilt before God and its implications for both the individual and for society. It talked about 'new birth for the individual and for society'.[35] The theological obscurity that surfaced here was to worsen in future conferences which had a purely social emphasis and scant respect for evangelism.

It was this kind of concern that prompted the German delegation to express its fear that the church was becoming secularized. They pointed to the creative act of God with which 'his kingdom will be consummated in the final establishment of a New Heaven and a New Earth.'[36] Sin, death and Satan are still real powers in our world, and we live as citizens of two different orders. It is Christ's prerogative, when he appears in power and glory, 'to transform the whole structure of this world into his kingdom of righteousness and victory'.[37] They emphasized that it was only the eschatological attitude that could prevent the church from becoming secularized.

The IMC merges with the WCC

With Tambaram's concern for evangelization receding into the background, the foundations had been laid for newer approaches to mission. Mission in its broader sense is now seen to be more than the activities of the traditional missionary; it is the role of the church itself. In view of such an emphasis, there was no longer any need for the IMC as a separate entity. Hence, at its Ghana meeting in 1957, the World Council of Churches was prepared to devour this missionary movement. The case for integration was so intelligently argued that many were led to believe that within the WCC the IMC was going to work miracles in stirring a much wider missionary concern.

But a significant group of leaders predicted that this convincing view of mission, as the church doing all that God's people were supposed to do, would not work out in practice. This concern was overwhelmed, however, by some forceful arguments for the theological correctness of the move.

It was pointed out that mission, as well as unity, belongs to the *esse* of the church. This is absolutely right. But the real issue is whether the WCC can claim to be the church. There is, even today, a definite need to restore mission to its rightful place within the church, but our understanding of the church itself also needs to be sharpened.

Max Warren, a strong voice in favour of biblical mission, rightly replied: 'Mission and Unity belong together, of course, but there is no obvious necessity for that belongingness to be stressed administratively.'[38] Admitting that he agreed with the position that mission can only be fulfilled in unity, he provocatively pointed out that

> in the providence of God, mission has been pursued in disunity. The two main groups, on the one hand the Pentecostals, on the other the Roman Catholics – neither of whom is particularly concerned with what we understand as unity – are the ones who are making the real, growing mission of the church today. These are the two groups who never ask about mission but get on with it.[39]

'Only in the pursuit of mission', said Warren, 'are we going to be led into the meaning of unity.'[40] Despite the convincing arguments for the 'belongingness' of mission in the essence of the church, mission was in danger of being consumed by the larger concerns of the ecumenical movement.

All attempts to caution the IMC about the dangers of merging with the WCC were in vain. At the Third Assembly of the WCC in New Delhi in 1961, the IMC, now integrated into the WCC, appeared in its new identity as the Commission and Division of World Mission and Evangelism (CWME). Rather than being realistically seen as only a department of the WCC, it was highlighted as 'the putting of the missionary obligation of the church right in the centre of the ecumenical movement'.[41] Sadly, and as the discerning had expected, the promise was not to be fulfilled. Instead, the passion soon went out of mission. When the church itself was seen as mission, traditional missionary activities were sidelined.

Mission reconceptualized

Subtle influences were now to appear. One can hardly believe that their effects were unintentional. Uppsala 1968, the Fourth Assembly of the WCC, was to capitalize on the centrality accorded to mission within the church and to make a powerful impact on belief about the nature of the church's mission. Mission was soon to be reconceptualized, with severe consequences. Missionary principles were to be re-evaluated and the church's role in the struggle for justice and liberation was to be accentuated.

The first document of the Assembly was entitled *The Church for Others*. The earlier church-centricism was to be discarded in favour of a more acceptable 'world-centricism'.[42] The tone of the proceedings was heavily dominated by social concerns rather than by evangelism. The changes that had taken place in between New Delhi and Uppsala in personnel, in emphasis and in direction now enabled the WCC to push ahead with vision and purpose.

> Formerly it was the IMC and its constituent members who were the experts on the mission of the church. Now . . . the logic was clear enough. If

the whole church was mission ... then every division of the WCC was competent to help discover what mission was. So instead of the CWME infusing the WCC with vision and passion for the unfinished missionary and evangelistic task, other divisions were slowly but steadily shaping the CWME to their concept of mission.[43]

Uppsala will be remembered for two major emphases which helped to reconceptualize mission. The first is the concept of 'humanization'. The goal of mission, traditionally seen as evangelization, was now to be understood as humanization. Mission was not to proselytize – that was outdated – but to communicate more relevantly 'in our period the meaning of the messianic goal'.[44]

In another day and age the goal of God's redemptive work might best have been described in terms of man turning towards God ... the fundamental question was that of the true God, and the church responded to that question by pointing to him. It was assumed that the purpose of mission was Christianization, bringing man to God through Christ and his church. Today the fundamental question is much more that of true man, and the dominant concern of the missionary congregation must therefore be to point to the humanity in Christ as the goal of mission.[45]

From Uppsala onwards, salvation is explored in terms of better relationships on a human level rather than in terms of relationship with God.

The God–world–church sequence

Uppsala's second emphasis was far more radical. The gist of the argument had already been published in *The Church for Others*:

> In the past it has been customary to maintain that God is related to the world through the church. When we sharpen this view into a formula the sequence would be: God–church–world. This has been understood to mean that God is primarily related to the church and only secondarily to the world by means of the church. Further, it has been held that God related himself to the world through the church in order to gather everyone possible from the world into the church. God, in other words, moves through the church to the world. We believe that the time has come to question this sequence and to emphasize an alternative. According to this alternative the last two items in God–church–world should be reversed, so that it reads God–world–church instead. That is, God's primary relationship is to the world and it is the world and not the church that is the focus of God's plan.[46]

It was argued that the old sequence of God–church–world tends to falsify the way God works in the world. A contradiction emerges. It was argued that mission belongs to the very essence of the church, yet almost with the same stroke it seems to have been asserted that mission does not belong to the church. Uppsala called for the removal of the ideas that God always initiates change from inside the church towards the 'outsiders' in the world. It attempted to lessen the emphasis on the church and thereby to show that God's activity was not confined there.[47]

God's activity is certainly worldwide, and it would be unbiblical to claim that he works only in the church. But the point at issue concerns the nature and function of the church. It has to do with the church's identity. Has not God chosen the church as the vehicle for his mission? Does the Bridegroom reject his Bride?

Our quest for a biblical foundation for mission will see the church as central in God's plan of action. The God–world–church sequence may sound attractive, but a closer look at the biblical understanding of mission, his election and covenant, will reveal the contrary. Not only does this sequence violate the biblical concept of mission; it even removes the necessity of the church from the plan of God. The secularization of mission allows the concerns of the world today to define what our mission must be. The church, and even the biblical framework of the outworking of God's purposes for the world today, become redundant.

With the shaking of the foundations of biblical mission, and the redefining of evangelism, evangelicals welcomed CWME's title for its 1973 conference in Bangkok as a sign of a hoped-for return to an emphasis on a biblical theme. But 'Salvation Today' was not to fulfil what the title seemed to promise. Bangkok was another attempt to redefine salvation, which completed the process begun at Uppsala. The secular and humanistic understanding of salvation reached its climax; mission was seen as having to do with all of human life.

Biblical mission must certainly impact all of life. If God is Lord of all, then he must work out his purposes for all. But the crucial question is: what is God's mission for all of human life? Is there any compelling message with which we are to go into the world, proclaiming a salvation the world does not have? Ironically, forces were working against all that the euphoric Edinburgh 1910 conference stood for. As Bangkok concluded, Emilio Castro, the then director of CWME, exclaimed: 'The Missionary era has ended and the era of World Mission has just begun.'[48]

2

Mission or missions?

When the ecumenical leaders gathered at Bangkok in 1973, the idea of salvation had come to encompass involvement in the struggle for human justice and dignity, in the struggle against alienation between people, and in the struggle between hope and despair in personal life. Salvation was now seen to be touching soul and body, the individual and society, humankind and the groaning creation. The secularized and action-oriented implications of the new view of mission challenged the traditional understanding of mission as evangelism.

The new concept of mission challenges not merely the traditional and conventional concept but also the biblical understanding itself. Christians will hardly deny that God is concerned for humankind as a whole, but can all involvement in human affairs be termed God's mission? 'If everything is mission,' observed Bishop Stephen Neill, 'nothing is mission, and we are back in the night in which all cats are grey.'[1]

Yet evangelicals need to accept that for far too long we have clung to an understanding of mission that perhaps does not fully correspond to our concept of God's lordship. If God is really Lord of all, then ought not his lordship to be demonstrated in wider terms than we have allowed? Ours has been an emphasis on a spiritual mission with little social concern. It is not that we have lacked social concern. There has been plenty. Take for instance our hospitals, schools, and aid to the poor. We have often tended, however, to see these purely as means of reaching the people with this spiritual gospel. Confronted by the broader implications of mission, we might want to retreat into an even more 'spiritual' understanding of it. Instead, as we reconsider our biblical mandate, we must accept that the fullest expression of the gospel involves fleshing it out to demonstrate in practical ways Christ's concern for a lost world.

As we look more closely at the new ecumenical direction of mission, we shall consider three particular implications, and in so doing seek to challenge our own limited understanding. The first aspect we note is a movement from the concept of missions to an understanding of mission. Second, we look at the shift away from the proclamation of the message of salvation to a plea for a dialogical approach. Third, we consider the shift from evangelization (sometimes labelled 'Christianization') to what is termed humanization. All these implications will assist us to draw out relevant biblical principles to undergird our biblical approach to mission today.

Mission, not missions

A key event that will help us to focus on the issues in their context is the integration of the International Missionary Council with the World Council of Churches, at which we glanced in chapter 1. This was finalized in New Delhi in 1961, although the decision had been made as far back as 1957. Although the IMC became just one division of the WCC, the claims about it were lofty. Christians were called to understand the intrinsic missionary character of their churchmanship and therefore not to permit any distinction between the church and its mission. Some greeted the merger warmly, while others discerned the probability that missionary intentions would be watered down.

The rationale behind the merger is noteworthy, although, one must hasten to add, the consequences have been unjustifiable. Edinburgh 1910 was a gathering of missionaries, mainly representatives of Western Protestant missionary agencies. Their aim was to renew the challenge to reach the millions who were still outside the church. Understandably in the triumphant times of Western imperialism, there also was the challenge to 'civilize' the worlds they would conquer. The fact that the era of missions had coincided with the era of Western cultural expansion is undeniable. In the light of these challenges it seemed appropriate and valid for Christians to reconsider the essence of mission.

Bishop Lesslie Newbigin, an enthusiast for the merger, summed up the essential elements of the new situation.

1. The political domination of the world by the white races has ended. The course of history is no longer determined by decisions made in Western capitals. Western culture as a whole is no longer accepted by the rest of the world as that which has the right and power to dominate and replace the cultures of Asia and Africa.

2. There is emerging a single world culture which has its characteristic expression in the rapidly growing cities in all parts of the world, and which has as its common substance the science and technology which have been developed in the West, and as its driving power the belief in the possibility of rational planning for total human welfare. This world culture is made possible by the existence of modern means of communication and transport.

3. The Christian church is now, for the first time, no longer confined to a small part of the earth, but is present – normally as a small minority – in almost all parts of the inhabited world.[2]

If we are to accept that there are no fixed patterns for mission, it seems reasonable to return to basics to find out how the church's mission, the mission of God, can be spelt out today. At Ghana 1957 the IMC had affirmed that world mission was Christ's, not ours. It had expressed a concern to free the course of God's mission to the world. That was probably a needed reminder.[3]

No Christian will deny that mission is truly God's. In WCC circles *missio Dei* has become the term to describe the thrust of God's mission. No longer is the stress on missionary agencies, missionaries and missions, in the sense of people going to 'mission fields'. This is what is meant by Emilio Castro's declaration, quoted at the end of the previous chapter, that the missionary era has ended. The one-way traffic has yielded to mission in a much wider sense. No longer is mission a matter of Western missionaries going to the pagan world, or of Christian countries sending missionaries to non-Christian countries. The day of *missions* has now given way to a day when *mission*, God's mission, will be fulfilled.

Basic to this view of mission is a concern that its direction must not continue to be from the Western 'home base' to the rest of the world. Consequently, the church was called to a newer understanding. Mission was to be

> concerned as the mission of the whole church to the whole world, with the implication that the church, wherever it exists and under whatever conditions it exists, is in principle part of the home base for mission to the ends of the earth, related in a nexus of mutual dependence and responsibility with every other part of the church in the fulfilment of that mission to the whole world.[4]

The argument thus far is convincing. As evangelicals we have ignored a basic biblical fact – the origin of mission in the heart of God himself, and the consequent necessity for the mission to be central in the character of the church – the entire church. Admittedly, our modern mission consciousness was aroused at a time of coldness to our missionary obligation, and 'missions' began with individuals concerned to respond to God's command. Missions became something of an optional involvement, an activity outside the church, with the church able only to support missions rather than being involved in mission. Now the focus shifts back to where it belongs – right at the heart of the church itself, burning with passion to be involved in the mission of God.

One healthy outcome of this renewed stress has been the attempt to understand the true nature of the church *vis-à-vis* the role of parachurch or mission agencies. Within the missionary-dominated period there seemed no need to define these structures, which had tended to be separate from the church. In fact, the relationship of church and missions has been an embarrassment in many instances. The surfacing of the need of the church to see mission as part of its essence is one positive outcome of the debate in recent times. The church itself expresses the mission of God, and, in fact, the church is mission.

The timing of the debate was right, because governments by and large have been questioning the role of 'foreigners' in the national church. The term 'missionary' has virtually become synonymous with 'westerner', and as a result mission smacks of a foreign intrusion. In Asia, with the resurgence of traditional religion, the threat of communalism, and wrongly motivated nationalism, the priority has been the rediscovery of the 'localness' of mission in the sense that every church and every country is part of the mission of God. This in itself could well have remedial effects on the explosive situations in some countries. A biblical theology of mission written anywhere today must seek to rediscover from the pages of the Bible the universality of mission, the width of God's concern for a lost world and the inescapable responsibility laid on every committed Christian to be involved in God's mission. In this sense the end of the 'missionary' era or the age of 'missions' is to be welcomed.

The task, then, is great. But what is biblical mission? What is God's mission? Is there no uniqueness in the message of the gospel? Is there any difference between mission in the past and mission today? These and several other questions need to be answered by evangelicals today. Naive responses will only demonstrate a lack of concern to build on the biblical foundation of which we boast.

Proclamation or dialogue?

These lofty claims about God's mission and the interpretation of the Christian message in the world today have a basic rationale – the accommodation of the gospel within a new environment. The optimism of the nineteenth century gradually gave way to a more sober assessment of Christian claims. Then there was the growing opposition from adherents of other religions. They had reacted to some naive and damaging perceptions of their beliefs. All this led to the call for a new attitude.

Rather than preaching down to the non-Christian, it became fashionable to talk about 'dialogue'. The age of conversions and Christian expansion had passed, it was claimed, and the new climate demanded a different approach. Some of the principles behind the plea can be summarized in the following assertions.[5]

1. We live in a pluralistic world in which many religions exist, and we have to learn to co-exist within limited areas. The only way to peace is for all to recognize the existence and the rights of all the rest.

2. This plurality of religions is likely to continue into a future extended as far as the human mind can see. The nineteenth-century expectation of the rapid disappearance of the non-Christian religions was based on a number of misconceptions, and cannot be seriously entertained today.

3. All religions bear witness at least in some measure to the presence and activity of God.

This used to be claimed only for the great historic religions. We now see that even the primal religions of Africa and such areas as the South Pacific are intricately woven textures, covering every aspect of the life of a people, and giving assurance of the presence and activity of God in every part of that life. In the past, history has been written in western categories only, and civilization has been identified simply and explicitly with western civilization. As a result, western people have tended to limit the idea of divine revelation, and claimed for Christianity a unique status as the one religion in which any gleam of divine truth can be discerned. Wider knowledge has made this claim untenable. After all, these other religions have sustained the inner life of millions of people over many centuries. Is it possible to affirm that God has had no hand at all in this, and that these different religions are nothing more than variant forms of error?

4. Christians who wish to enter into dialogue with those of other faiths must resolutely put away every thought of intellectual, religious or cultural superiority, as though dialogue were a one-way traffic in which communication of truth would be from their side alone. Such an attitude is a relic of the old western superiority complex, and renders impossible from the start any dialogue on terms of equality and mutual comprehension.

5. The Christian must firmly put away the idea that it is his or her business to 'bring Christ' to the non-Christian. It is part of Christian belief that God has reconciled the whole world to himself in Christ, and that since the resurrection Christ is present everywhere in the world that he has redeemed. The non-Christian is

part of this redeemed world. Therefore, Christ is already present in the other whom we meet. The Christian comes not to bring Christ but to find him, though he or she may also be privileged to bring more clearly into the consciousness of the other the Christ who is already in him.

6. Christians must approach the interlocutor in the hope of gaining more than they have to give. They should go in the expectation that the other has more of God than Christians have themselves, and that they, the Christians, will end the encounter with their awareness of God amplified and enriched.

7. There must be no question of conversion from one faith to another. Each person must be encouraged to go forward to the highest level of attainment possible on the path on which he or she has already set out. Conversion has undesirable consequences in social and emotional disruption, and these are likely to harm rather than help the development of true spiritual life.

We need have no doubt about the rightness of dialogue. Two-way communication has always been essential, and it is possible to see attempts at dialogue even within the life of the early church. Our one-way attitude in communicating the gospel has resulted in a sad lack of awareness of other viewpoints, whether right or wrong. We have lacked that sensitivity which could have resulted in greater effectiveness in our communication.

The crucial question, however, is: what do we mean by 'dialogue'? What are we trying to achieve?

Mainstream Christians have usually adopted one of two attitudes to other religions, and these attitudes have defined their understanding of dialogue. These two positions are referred to as *exclusivism* and *inclusivism*.

The first of these, exclusivism, maintains that one's religion is the only true religion. It then follows naturally that all other religious viewpoints are false. This position produces an absolute commitment to proclaim one's religion despite charges of intolerance and contempt. This was clearly the early church's position, and by and large it is still maintained by the conservative Protestant church and the evangelical community.

The second term, inclusivism, describes the belief that there are different levels of truth in all religions and one must reinterpret one's own truth to be compatible with all other truths. Each religion will then develop a vision that will embrace others in tolerance and magnanimity. This inclusive attitude still enables the believer to maintain his claim to the truth, but also allows him to include other truths within his system. This position is that of the Roman Catholic Church and also that of liberal Protestants. Many recent studies have sought to develop this position in the light of mission.

Raimundo Panikkar's widely acclaimed book *The Unknown Christ of Hinduism* is a fervent cry for dialogue, and challenges the church to take dialogue seriously.

> If Christianity, on the one hand, aspires to be the universal religion, what is the meaning of any encounter it may have with Hinduism? Where and how can Hinduism take up the challenge of the nature and presence of Christianity? If, on the other hand, Hinduism claims to be the *sanathana dharma*, the highest 'everlasting religion', how can it start a true dialogue with Christianity? Is there any way for Christianity to cope with such a claim?[6]

Panikkar calls for interpenetration between the faiths. As the term suggests, this attitude to dialogue allows for interaction with one another and thereby supplements one's belief with whatever is found helpful. This is neither exclusivism nor inclusivism, but a mutual interpenetration which does not result in losing one's own distinctives.

Wishing to ignore fundamentalist attitudes and fanaticisms, Panikkar advocates a position which he claims will neither dilute the nature of Christianity nor do Hinduism an injustice. He rejects the 'substitution of one religion for the other',[7] which he sees as the Christian 'missionary attitude', as being dishonest and contrary to the principles of Christianity.

Panikkar wants the kind of attitude that does not imply a 'rivalry between the two religions'[8] but addresses 'the relationship between the deepest faith of the followers of the Vedic tradition and a faith which Christians cannot help but call '"Christian"'.[9] He clarifies this when he says that 'we must refrain from rejecting a religious text or tradition – an attitude that has often proved fatal – simply because it does not accord with our already crystallized ideas or formulations.'[10]

Panikkar's sensitivity is evident when he declares that even his use of the word 'Christ' does not imply any 'Christian imperialism'. It is rather the name Christians use to express the reality common to all religions; but there is 'no monopoly on the name or any form of exclusivity'. For him, God is at work in all religions, and 'the Christian kerygma does not proclaim a new God, but the *mirabilia* of God of which the Mystery of Christ hidden in God is the *alpha* and *omega*'. 'In the wake of St Paul we believe we may speak not only of the unknown God of the Greeks, but also of the *hidden Christ of Hinduism* – hidden and unknown and yet present and at work because he is not far from any one of us.'[11] He concludes that 'recognizing the presence of *God* in other religions is equivalent to proclaiming the presence of Christ in them, "for in him all things subsist"'.[12]

On this reasoning, dialogue becomes an effort to discover the Christ that is already there in Hinduism rather than a superior claim to offer Christ to the Hindu. We approach Hindus on equal terms and are even in a position of learning from them rather than showing the judgmental attitude we are criticized for having demonstrated previously.

The present-day challenge, however, takes us even further away from the issues of exclusivism and inclusivism. It is an urgent challenge to adopt a positive attitude to other religions, seeing them all as valid. No longer can we hold an idea of uniqueness that will challenge other religious positions. In our world, being torn apart by various forces, Christians are called to seek a mutuality that will result in harmony. This position is referred to as *pluralism*, the acceptance not only of the existence of all the religious paths but also of their vitality, their influence in our modern world, their depth, beauty and attractiveness.[13] This new attitude to the pluralistic environment with which we have already become familiar is gaining much ground. It brings with it a challenge to engage in dialogue with a totally open attitude.

The object of the exercise is to display tolerance, yet at the same time to continue to affirm the essence of the Christian gospel. Stephen Neill makes a caustic comment:

> It has often surprised me that Christians alone should be required to be tolerant in a world in which no-one else is prepared to be tolerant. The dedicated Marxist regards himself as a man with a mission. He alone knows the truth about society and about the ways in which society changes; all other men walk blindly in the world of ideology. His sincerity demands that he should be a ferocious propagandist; the greater the sincerity, the greater the ferocity. The Muslim is equally of the opinion that he has the whole truth . . . To the Buddhist there is only one way . . . All these are propagandist religions and make no secret of it.[14]

In our search for a theology of mission, we have already affirmed that we seek a biblical foundation. The Bible is clear about the terms on which we approach other religions. There is a finality to the message of Jesus Christ and we must maintain that. This does not mean, however, that we disregard dialogue as unbiblical. Naive arguments for preaching as the only way of communicating the gospel need to be questioned. Evangelicals must shake off suspicions that all dialogue smacks of compromise, universalism and a weakening of the evangelistic task. A dialogical approach could open many more doors for the proclamation of the gospel. Although we present Christ as the only Saviour, we are biblically justified in using any possible means to make known the message of the kingdom.

Paul's proclamation of the gospel, for instance, displays an admirable adaptability to the varying situations he addresses. With Jewish audiences he drew heavily on their own past and established points of contact with their own belief. With the Greeks at Athens he appealed to their educated minds, demonstrating his familiarity with their traditions, which he used in support of his arguments. He became 'all things to all men so that by all possible means I might save some' (1 Cor. 9:22).

Paul did not merely want to build bridges, however. All his effort to find 'entry points' was directed towards the confrontation with Christ that was to follow. Those who believe that Paul regretted his cautious presentations at Lystra and Athens, and determined to confront people directly with the crucified Christ as in his preaching at Corinth, have a strong case.

All this points to the fact that there is no biblical justification for a dialogue that will assist the non-believer to discover salvation in his own traditions and beliefs. The concepts of the 'hidden Christ' and the 'anonymous Christian' are an outright betrayal of biblical portrayals of Jesus Christ and his message. The emphasis on dialogue does, however, remind us that we should indeed approach people of other religions. We need to seek new direction in the Bible as we face our present-day context.

Humanization, not evangelization

Mission, as it was being reconceptualized in the WCC, was being opened up to become all that it was supposedly intended to be. Philip Potter, the first Third World head of the WCC, enumerates four consequences of the newer insights of this mission.

> In the first place, the church as the people of God is not the centre and goal of mission, but the means and instrument. The church participates in God's mission, in what God is doing in the world . . . As Christ took the form or structure proper to God's purpose, so the church must adapt its forms and structures to God's mission today as during every period in history.[15]

Potter suggests that this understanding compels us to reconsider three attitudes we have towards mission: (a) the tendency to equate the church with the kingdom of God, rather than to see it as a sign of the kingdom; (b) the tendency, by speaking of 'our mission', to force those whom we seek to evangelize into our patterns of thinking and living; and (c) the tendency to regard our historically conditioned structures as fixed, sacred and indispensable to the fulfilment of God's mission. Potter's observation could well serve as a valid reminder about the need to demonstrate sensitivity both to the text and to the context of our proclamation.

When we come to Potter's second consequence of the new insights into mission, however, we begin to discern his broader concern.

> If the drama of mission is God's involvement with the world, the church must take with radical seriousness what is happening in that world. Mission may not mean giving the church's answers to

its own questions. Christ himself showed deep concern for listening to people's questions before he deepened those questions and gave his answer in word and deed ... We must listen to the world's agenda.[16]

We must take this caution seriously too, but the crucial issue is how we act upon it.

The third consequence of the new conception of mission, Potter reminds us, is to accept that 'the whole world is the mission field, not just what have traditionally been called non-Christian countries'.[17] Again, we should have no problem with this, and in fact should accept it as positively biblical. The problem arises, however, when we are asked to accept that 'the new humanity which is God's missionary purpose is the quest of every continent and country'.[18]

Potter's fourth consequence of the new ideas of mission clarifies this statement.

The church which participates in God's mission as the servant body of Christ and takes the world's agenda seriously is itself being renewed to be the sign of the new humanity. The church as the people of God never remains static in the process of mission. Mission is not only concerned with the conversion of others but with the conversion of God's people.[19]

Hence, Potter concludes, because the survival of humanity is a priority on the world's agenda, the church has an inescapable responsibility in this area.

We have no reason to reject Potter's concerns outright, particularly since we are called to an 'ever greater depth of involvement in the tragedy of the world's disobedience and rebellion and their need for turning to God and receiving afresh his renewing grace'.[20] Our problem begins, however, when we notice Potter's one-sided emphasis. He goes on: 'Life before and with God means practising justice and being devoted to loyal kindness to all.'[21] He argues that Jesus Christ was made man in order to 'show how human beings can practise justice and show this kindness to the poor, the oppressed, the alienated, as expressions of life in and with God'.[22] Potter sums up: 'Negatively, this means working for the survival of humanity. Positively, it means entering into the struggle for fulness of life in justice and peace.'[23]

This renewal that mission is to receive subtly but completely shifts the focus from God to humanity. It is a secular humanistic focus that can easily fit within our modern-day environment with no danger of converting the heathen to the Christian faith.

Two concerns lay behind this new shift. First, there was an attack on rigid and tradition-bound church structures which had resulted in a church-centred rather than a Christ-centred mission. The Dutch theologian Johannes Hoekendijke had pleaded for a 'church for others' wherein 'mobilizing the people of God for mission today means releasing them from structures that inhibited them in the church'.[24]

Hoekendijke was right to point out the fallacy of making the church the starting-point and goal of mission.

> Would it not be a good thing [he pleaded] to start all over again in trying to understand what it really means when we repeat again and again our favourite missionary text, 'the gospel of the kingdom will be proclaimed throughout the *oikoumenē*', and attempt to rethink our ecclesiology within this framework of kingdom–gospel–apostolate–world?[25]

The challenge is to stop looking at the world from within the church, to break out of such bondages, and to redefine mission in the context of the world itself. The shift is not only away from the church but ultimately away from the Bible as well, as the context will now begin to dominate our definitions.

There is no problem in accepting that we need to take a fresh look at our ecclesiology. Static, denominational and structural understandings have undoubtedly stifled mission. Mission was, at best, merely one activity forced into this structure, while liturgical concerns were more essential to our understanding of the church. Distinguishing between a Christ-centred mission and a church-centred one, however, creates problems. The kind of Christ-centred mission advocated by Hoekendijke and others has a foothold in the world and only a vague, idealistic allegiance to Christ. Biblically based and church-centred mission ought to be Christ-centred mission.

The second concern behind this new shift to humanization is also a reaction against an inadequate understanding of evangelism. Sometimes we have equated evangelism with the numerical growth of the church. Some recent church growth approaches could be subtly conditioned by this inadequate understanding. Further, evangelism has been equated with 'crusade-type' preaching. Numerous evangelists, having witnessed the Spirit-anointed success of Billy Graham, attempt to press themselves into that mould in the belief that evangelism consists only of that style of mass proclamation. Then there is the kind of evangelism that has so concentrated on saving souls that any practical implications of the gospel have been shunned as belonging to liberal theology.

It is, then, hardly surprising that we have been challenged to widen our understanding of mission. The WCC reconceptualization from the perspective of the world cannot, however, be biblically justified. The amendment of 'God–church–world' to 'God–world–church' has some threatening implications. It invites us to relate our theology to the varying needs of the world without any absolutes to correct our thinking. Although mission is loftily described as God's mission, in the end it turns out to be what human beings conceptualize. This preoccupation with the world without the authority of the Word is tantamount to the secularizing of mission. God does not seem to be the centre any more.

With such a perspective on mission, evangelization in its traditional, biblical sense becomes no longer acceptable. Potter considered himself committed to evangelism, but the real issue is, 'What is evangelism?' Setting people free from human bondages, from dehumanizing structures, and from exploitative and oppressive forces, becomes the prime concern, rather than offering people a right relationship to God.

Uppsala set the tone for the 'renewal' of mission and opened wide the door for everything the church does to be termed 'mission'. With the emphasis shifted from reconciliation between God and man to reconciliation between man and man the foundation of Christian mission is shaken. A well-known WCC General Secretary, W. A. Visser't Hooft, put it aptly:

> There is a great tension between the vertical interpretation of the gospel as essentially concerned with God's saving action in the life of individuals and the horizontal interpretation of it as mainly concerned with human relationships in the world. A Christianity that has lost its vertical dimension has lost its salt, and is not only insipid but useless for the world.[26]

Such a clear caution as this could be seen as an attack on the position of one of the WCC's strongest advocates of 'humanization', M. M. Thomas. Thomas sees even the concept of salvation itself as in need of replacement. In his well-known booklet *Towards a Theology of Contemporary Ecumenism*, he states:

> Salvation itself could be defined as humanization in a total eschatological sense. And all our

struggles on earth for the fragmentary realization of man's humanity point to this eschatological humanization as their judgment and fulfilment.[27]

Three years later in Bangkok he affirmed this even more clearly:

> Herein lies the mission of the church: it is to participate in the movements of human liberation of our time in such a way as to witness to Jesus Christ as the Source, the Judge and the Redeemer of the human spirituality and its orientations as it is at work in these movements, and therefore as the Saviour of man today.[28]

Visser't Hooft's cautions are to be heeded as we see the thoroughly horizontal dimension of mission being propagated overwhelmingly. This understanding of mission is far from biblical. Sunand Sumithra, in his definitive study of Thomas's theology, points out the purely secular nature of his approach.

> [Thomas's] understanding of mission is basically political . . . his emphasis on the confession of participation as against proclamation, humanization as the goal, and Jesus Christ understood as the unifier, the ideal, an historical understanding of the kingdom of God rather than the apocalyptic, the emphasis on the function of the church rather than her nature – to mention a few – all these reveal this political aspect.[29]

While we evangelicals do need to open our own eyes to some broader dimensions of mission, it is also true that in recent years the WCC has become open to a far more positive attitude to evangelism. While this has been largely due to pressure from a number of their members who continue to affirm the centrality of the gospel of Jesus Christ, it has also come from a growing respect for the conservative Protestant and evangelical position. The pressure of pluralism, however, has begun to demand even more openness to other religions.

We must stress that God's mission must be allowed to exercise its influence in every area of life. We must develop the implications of God's lordship over all his creation, which itself is sufficient to underline the fact that his mission must be concerned with all that is under that lordship. But if we remove the vertical relationship (God to people) and allow mission to be dictated purely by horizontal relationships (person to person), we are left with merely human mission. If this mission is neither anchored in the Bible, nor channelled through the church, it becomes a purely relative, human endeavour.

This criticism, however, does not sanction the preoccupation of some evangelicals with the vertical dimension to the exclusion of the horizontal. Visser't Hooft added that 'a Christianity that would use the vertical dimension as a means of escape from its responsibility in the common life of man is a denial of the incarnation of God's love for the world manifested in Christ'.[30] The challenge is obvious. As well as stressing the primacy of evangelism in the mission of the church, we urgently need to explore the biblical implications for mission that would lead naturally to the horizontal dimension. Humanization is not unbiblical. Mankind is dehumanized in the sense that we have not allowed God to make us all that we were intended to be. It is as a result of human sin that dehumanizing tendencies are embedded within our world. God is concerned for the real world, for real human beings, and for mission that will not merely touch one aspect of his world but that will make an impact on all of it.

Our discussions so far have helped us to grasp the problem we deal with when we talk about mission today. There is an urgent need to restore a biblical perspective that will correct the secular humanistic tendencies within the mission ascribed to the biblical God. As we restore this perspective, we may discover any restrictions we have imposed on the church's mission – restrictions that will detract from a full understanding of God's kingdom concern for the world today.

PART 2

A biblical exploration of mission

3

The Old Testament foundation

In commencing our study of the biblical foundations of mission we face enormous new challenges. No longer can we afford to repeat the theological systematizations that have been handed down to us. We must come to the Bible with our own, new situation in mind. We need have no problem in seeking a fresh theology, for if we truly believe that the Bible has eternal relevance, we should find that it speaks our situation today. To allow the Bible to speak is our task as we write a theology of mission.

Two points are worth making at the outset. First, we are dealing with a theology of *mission*. Hence this study is restricted to those theological considerations that have missiological implications. The task can be as challenging and fresh as we want it to be. New insights into familiar biblical themes may emerge as we approach mission from a biblical perspective.

An explanation may be necessary. Seeking to write a fresh theology of mission in no way implies a liberal attitude to the Bible. The Bible is the authoritative revelation of God. But we are concerned with the interpretation of that revelation – with hermeneutics. Passages that had relevance in one particular context must be transposed into our present context, and we must attempt to merge the two horizons in order to formulate a theology that will be biblical as well as contextualized.

Secondly, we are attempting to lay a *biblical* foundation for missiology. This further restricts our study to biblical insights, based on the belief that the Bible is the authoritative Word of God which was revealed in particular historical contexts. It is our task to transpose that revelation from the biblical context to our context today. The understanding that results from the interaction between the original and the present contexts will provide a theology of mission that will be both biblical and contextualized. This is to theologize with missiological intentions.

In recent hermeneutical studies, there have been attempts to bring about an interpretation based on the mediation between the 'then' and the 'now'. One significant example is that of the German philosopher Hans-Georg Gadamer in his concept of the 'two horizons'.[1] He clearly distinguishes between the two horizons – that of the past and that of the present. The past is a fixed horizon, whereas our present one – the interpreter's position – is capable of movement. As the interpreter tries to relate the strange horizon of the past to the present, a new horizon is formed as the two horizons merge.

It behoves us to have a more positive attitude to the past. Hermeneutical study should be a matter of entering into the past event and seeking to relate it to the present context. The past becomes part of the present. Gadamer emphasizes the need for a 'prejudice' or a 'presupposition' which we will inject into this process, and for the purposes of our study this is the process of theologizing for mission. Critical of 'prejudice against prejudice' – the Enlightenment attitude that sought 'pure facts' without biased interpretations – Gadamer seeks to restore a positive attitude to mission in its fullest expression, showing that there can be no 'presuppositionless' interpretation.

Following Gadamer, with our own correctives where necessary, we can approach our task of interpreting the biblical events in a positive manner. Mission must be seen as the activity of a living God working in actual history. Hence, our theology of mission is no vague theologizing. It is the actual historicity of the past event, plus the authority of its character as revelation, that gives us the basis of our theological consideration for mission today.

It has been heartening to see that recent approaches to a theology of mission have delved right back into the Old Testament. This is a valuable corrective to approaches that were restricted to the New Testament and a few well-worn passages in the Old. No theology of mission is complete without substantial reference to God's eternal purposes as revealed right from the start. Jesus Christ came not to abolish the old covenant but to bring to a climax all the expectations of the people of God as recorded from Genesis to Malachi. Theologies of mission that start with the New Testament lack the firm and full foundation of God's mission as it has been gradually revealed right from creation.

Sometimes, however, the Old Testament has been over-emphasized in support of one-sided theologies of mission. Rather than just negatively criticizing such treatments, we must positively lay an adequate and consistent foundation on which we can build a biblical theology of mission for today. As we endeavour to lay a holistic theological foundation, we shall be compelled to span the breadth of the biblical narrative and will thus come to appreciate the depth of God's mission.

The presupposition on which we build our theology of mission is that God has an ultimate plan for his world and that this plan relates to his kingdom. Although we have a limited insight into this plan at present, the Bible heavily underlines the fact that God is working out his ultimate purposes despite the contrary forces that are at work at the same time.

Relating this to our discussion earlier, we are really confronted with three, not two, horizons. Our foundational horizon is that of the past, the revelation of God as recorded in the Bible. As faithfully as possible, we are to draw out of this horizon all that is relevant for our understanding today. But there is also the horizon of the future, the culmination of the history of God's dealings with humanity and its world, the ultimate consummation of God's kingdom. In our study of mission we must constantly keep before us this ultimate perspective, the horizon of the future. The merging of these two horizons, of the past and of the future, with our own horizon in the present, will help us to understand God's mission to the world today.

In the constant interaction between the horizons, our own horizon will also be continuously expanding. Why restrict ourselves to fixed interpretations, as if a total revelation of God were available to us? We need to see God's action not merely in the past, the present or the future, but in the interaction of all of these.

Creation

When we adopt a redemption perspective on theology, we tend to go back only as far as the fall. In contrast, a creation theology will complete our picture of God's concern for mankind. Since creation, not the fall, marks the start of God's dealings with mankind, it makes sense to begin our study of God's mission there. A truly holistic perspective, a total sweep of God's revelation, must have some beginning. We shall therefore consider some aspects of the doctrine of creation that will assist us in commencing our study of God's mission.

The biblical teaching about creation stands in contrast to all primitive depictions. It emphasizes the one who creates with a purpose to be fulfilled. Creation is primarily the personal will of God. God intends mankind to live in an environment that he created, rather than in an environment that is alien to God's purposes. The negative attitude to the material world stemming from both Greek and Hindu thought needs to be dispelled as we note that God himself sees his creation as 'good' (Gn. 1:31). 'Good' means not only that it is right and proper, but that it is meaningful, beautiful and purposeful. God wants the very best for mankind, and so he prepares the best possible environment for them.

God's total mission

Creation, even in its organic and material sense, is the vehicle by which God chooses to reveal his glory. This truth, particularly, helps to counteract the tendency in Hinduism to dissolve historicity within the cosmic dimensions of religion. In Hinduism, reality and salvation are to be found in an escape or detachment from creation and history, not experienced in them. In contrast to the idea that creation is only a hindrance to spiritual reality, the God of the Bible reveals himself through a good and meaningful creation which demonstrates God's intricate design for his ultimate glory.

In stressing God's revelation through his creation we do not in any way intend to displace mankind from the centre of that creation. With our concern to be biblical, there is hardly any need to stress the centrality of mankind in God's redemptive purposes. Humanity's fallenness is God's primary concern. We must correct stress on the horizontal dimension of mission (our need for reconciliation with others, with ourselves and with our environment) by means of an adequate stress on the vertical. God's mission starts with the vertical concern. God wants to reconcile mankind to himself, and all other aspects of reconciliation revolve around this. In our attempt to restore a positive attitude to creation, however, we seek to demonstrate that mission is an activity of God in a real world and not something opposed to the material. Depicting humanity as struggling to escape an evil creation not only contradicts the goodness and purposefulness of creation but also insults the God who is responsible for it. In fact, mission is God himself entering into our world and seeking to restore us and our environment to the glory that God intended.

Even though mankind is the climax of creation, however, it is only a part of God's total creation. As if to underline this fact, God reminds us, 'Dust you are and to dust you will return' (Gn. 3:19). This not merely indicates human temporality; it depicts our link with the rest of creation. We are not independent of other created things, but live in interdependence with them. Nothing that God makes is in isolation from the rest of his creation. God's mission must be seen in its totality as concern for humanity and all the rest of God's creation.

In a day when ecological concerns confront us forcefully, a fresh look at the Bible will help us to restore a positive attitude to creation. This does not mean that we will become subservient worshippers of creation, but we do need to develop a healthy respect for God's world. God, having created the world, will certainly continue to care for it. By overemphasizing the fact that the world was made for mankind we have tended to exploit the world – probably the root of the ecological problem.

The important fact that is beginning to emerge is that God's mission to mankind is not independent of God's mission to creation. A truly biblical belief in creation must be translated into a concern for God's total created order. The interdependence of mankind and its environment is only now being recognized as the ecological devastation awakens us to deeper dimensions of our stewardship. God's mission is not for mankind alone. Sin has affected the whole of creation, and hence all creation, including men and women, must be the object of God's redemption.

We now begin to see the restrictions we evangelicals have previously imposed on our understanding of mission. We used to speak of our concern for 'the salvation of souls'. To be fair, we did not really mean that it was only the soul that was important. But because we have been influenced heavily by the Platonic concept of the immortality of souls, it seemed natural to emphasize the soul. Our mission has been slow to accept any material dimensions of salvation. But God's dealings with mankind are set within the fulness of his creation itself, and his ultimate plans envelop all of his handiwork.

Moreover, when we begin our study with creation, we see that mission is directed at the whole of humanity. We realize that humanity's history commences with God's interest in humanity *per se* and not just with Hebrew humanity. God's interest in humanity is not restricted to one particular race. He chose a particular race in order to demonstrate his purposes for all of his creation. There has always been a universality to God's mission. We have conveniently ignored the universalism that is implied in

God's concern for humanity as a whole. The inhuman separation between people on grounds of caste, colour and even religion needs to be corrected in the light of a creator God who is Lord over all, and whose mission extends to all, regardless of their background.

The never-ending debate on the relationship between evangelism and social action has been dealt with from varied perspectives, mostly in a defensive way. Evangelicals have argued for the priority of evangelism while liberals have stressed social action. The only true solution will come when we begin to approach the parts from the perspective of the whole rather than the other way around. When we start from creation we are able to approach the apparent tension between the two from the perspective of God's concern for the whole. The same will apply when we look at the problem from the perspective of God's ultimate plan. Seen from this fullest perspective, we will find it hard to restrict God's influence to merely one aspect of human need.

We need to be more fully involved in human need than we have been. We have in fact constricted our understanding of the dealings of God. It is true that only our relationship to Jesus Christ teaches us the primacy of evangelism. Limiting our study of God's mission to creation will not reveal this to us. It is for this reason that we constantly need to have before us the horizons that provide a meaningful understanding of, and holistic involvement in, mission. The doctrine of creation reminds us that God's desire is for the salvation of mankind, but not at the expense of his widest concerns for everything that he has created.

Historicity and culture

A deeper understanding of creation also enables us to correct false views of spirituality which have robbed God's mission of its rightful place within a concrete historical context. For instance, the Hindu view of detachment as the ultimate goal stems primarily from an inadequate view of creation. The *sanyasin*, considered to be the ideal man, 'spends his days in contemplation, pondering over the mysteries of life ... the free man of the spirit, who has broken through the narrow circles of clan and country. He has nothing to accomplish in this world or the next ... and so the entire choir of heaven and furniture of the earth seem naught before his divine vision'.[2] The popular practice of yoga, for instance, is seen as a means of detachment from the material world, true, pure consciousness being spiritual. Asia needs to be confronted with the biblical God of the material universe, and with a spirituality that recognizes God within that real world.

Closely linked with God's concern for a material world, in which all humanity has the potential to receive his redemptive benefits, is the issue of culture. We are not concerned here with an elaborate discussion of culture, but merely state that the God of creation must ultimately be the God of human culture. Culture is the sum total of visible and invisible characteristics that first of all distinguish humankind from beasts and secondly distinguish groups of people from one another. Mankind in God's image, with the potential of creativity and the freedom within which he has been privileged to express this creativity, will naturally tend to express himself in concrete forms as well as abstract attitudes. Art, dance and music (for example) are the crowning glory of such expressions, but all these are relevant within a particular milieu of actions, words, attitudes, customs and habits. God, having made mankind autonomous within his creative order, must assume the final responsibility for culture, although this does not imply that he fully accepts it as pure and holy.

Because of the fall, all culture is tainted with sin. There is still, however, sufficient basis for us to see culture as one aspect of the expression of the image of God in mankind, which seeks to actualize itself in concrete and visible expressions that materially hold mankind together in God's created world. God's involvement in creation itself could be seen as the inauguration of culture. He wanted form and order; he wanted goodness and beauty; he ultimately wanted mankind to reside in an attractive environment, and even gave mankind the autonomy to carry on this cultural involvement. The man was to name the creatures as he chose; he could rule over them; he could multiply them as he saw fit.

This positive acceptance of culture is necessary first of all to dispel any wrong attitudes that have obstructed a truly incarnational mission. Some have naively come to believe that there is such a thing as a universal Christian culture which stands in opposition to local, non-Christian cultures. Sometimes, the culture handed down by western missionaries (often, but usually unintentionally, smacking of western culture), has been identified with 'Christian culture'.

As we have already noted, as well as evaluating culture positively, we must accept the need for God's judgment on culture. God's responsibility for creation did not cease when he created mankind. It continues even after the fall, and hence fallen mankind with a fallen culture is also his concern. The fall opened the door to direct and indirect satanic influences on culture. If we accept the reality of the fall, we must also accept that no culture is perfect and altogether good. The cultures of this world are also part of God's total redemptive concern as they are shaped and moulded in accordance with the ultimate kingdom culture.

Mankind and its environment

Added to God's widest concern for mankind, we must recognize God's concern for mankind's world. While there is no doubt that mankind is the crowning event of creation, we restrict God's purposes if we restrict his concern to mankind. Recognizing the essential goodness of creation must lead us to recognize that God purposefully created the right environment for mankind. It was a 'very good' creation, through which he was to reveal his glory. We urgently need to develop a correct perspective on mankind within this God-created environment in order to develop a proper attitude towards that environment.

Christians have been attacked for their arrogance towards creation, which has resulted in the exploitation of the material world.[3] The ecological crisis, viewed as a theological problem, will help us to look carefully at the biblical attitude towards creation. The Bible clearly allows no exploitation of creation. Our stewardship of creation has been misinterpreted and has resulted in mismanagement of it. A respect for creation will correct environmental exploitation. Yet we must guard against the exaggerated respect that leads to the worship of nature. A healthy respect for creation must point to the creator God behind creation's beauty and wonder. God, desiring the best for mankind, planned a meaningful existence within a purposeful world which he created for his glory.

The broadening of the scope of mission is linked with our particular understanding of mission. There should be no argument against the fact that God is ultimately Lord of all that he has created. But the question is how far we allow this fact to influence our understanding of mission. Some limit God's mission to God's interest in mankind's salvation. In our attempts to define mission, however, we must consider God's ultimate concern to establish his kingdom. This demands that we look at mankind within its God-made environment, and accept that if God has created both mankind and this environment, he is surely concerned for all that he has created. Perhaps we are really talking about much more than God's mission. It is God's concern for all of his creation – a kingdom concern.

The doctrine of creation both roots mission in history and sets mankind within the perspective of that creation. Because God's concern is so wide, we must see his mission as wide also. Perhaps we should think of a scaling down of operations from God's perspective through the church's perspective and right down to the individual's perspective. At its highest, then (that is in God's perspective), mission cannot be anything less than the totality of God's concern.

Jesus Christ and creation

Paul speaks of creation being 'subjected to frustration, not by its own choice, but by the will of the one who subjected it, in hope that the creation itself will be liberated from its bondage to decay' (Rom. 8:20–21). Christian mission, if it must develop in greater sensitivity to God's total concern, must develop a truly ecological concern. The relationship between mankind and its environment highlights the intensity of Paul's imagery when he says that even creation 'waits in eager expectation for the sons of God to be revealed' (Rom. 8:19). We must focus not only on mankind's redemption but also on the interdependence between mankind and its environment. In so doing we must encourage a more positive attitude to our God-given environment and to whatever redemption means to God's non-human creation.

Creation is in fact so important to God that along with proclaiming Jesus Christ's authority over the church, Paul re-emphasizes Christ's authority over creation. 'For by him all things were created: things in heaven and on earth, visible and invisible . . . all things were created by him and for him. He is before all things, and in him all things hold together' (Col. 1:16–17). New Testament Christians are able to see the centrality of Christ in God's creation. If he is central in creation, it must follow that to speak of Jesus' mission to mankind without reference to Jesus' concern for the whole of creation is to disregard a key part of God's mission.

The church must explore the full meaning of the lordship of Christ within the wide framework of his redemptive mission. The psalmist demonstrates this complete view of God's redemptive purposes when he calls on us to 'Sing to the LORD a new song' (Ps. 96:1–2). It is a song that proclaims the purpose of creation: his salvation extends to all nations (verses 2–3) – reminding us that 'the LORD reigns' and that the world is firmly established (verse 10). His whole creation must rejoice (verse 11), for the Lord will fulfil his purposes as he comes to judge the earth in

righteousness and truth (verse 13). The universal implications of mission do not imply universalism but rather
emphasize the universal availability of salvation.

We have yet to deal with the purpose of creation as far as
mankind is concerned. It is not enough to say, as we have
already done, that creation is for God's glory. This could be
just as unbalanced as the kind of spirituality we have tried
to avoid. A thorough reading of the Old Testament would
reveal this answer:

> He has created it for the covenant, that is to say
> because of his plan of love and salvation for
> humanity by means of Israel. In creating the
> world God already had the covenant in view, and
> it is this motive which gave to the idea of creation
> its specific orientation.[4]

This understanding stands against dualistic conceptions
that separate God from mankind and creation. Yet, at the
same time, it accords autonomy to creation and to mankind. 'This autonomy . . . makes possible a covenant.'[5] It is
plain that a covenant can be made only between two autonomous parties. The biblical account of creation highlights
a lofty view of God, yet it does not reduce mankind to
pawns in God's hands.

Sin and salvation can be understood only when this
autonomy is appreciated. Moreover, God's mission to
mankind becomes all the more meaningful when we grasp
this. The fact that God makes a covenant imposes no
restrictions on him. In his sovereignty he is free to act as he
wills. Yet the establishing of a covenant between God and
mankind and creation points to an interdependence
between the two parties. Paul ascribes this holding
together of all God's creation to Jesus Christ, by whom 'all
things hold together' (Col. 1:17). All that God has created
is good and accordingly belongs together. Sin causes divisions in creation, but it is God's will that in Christ all things
should be reconciled. Mission therefore expresses the

heart of God who wants all things to come together in Jesus Christ. 'For God was pleased to have all his fulness dwell in him, and through him to reconcile to himself all things, whether things on earth or things in heaven, by making peace through his blood, shed on the cross' (Col. 1:19–20).

We shall develop this theme of Jesus Christ and creation more fully in chapter 7.

Election

We have already commented on the negative view of the church's role in mission. We noted the argument that the church as an institution has failed to carry out its responsibility. This resulted in mission being portrayed in a God–world–church perspective, on the ground that the church can no longer claim to be the channel of God's mission to the world. Despite the fact that the church may have failed, however, one cannot dismiss its role without a fresh look at the role of the church as depicted in the Bible. In dealing with the theme of election and God's people in the Old Testament, we are able to consider a valuable corrective to this wrong emphasis.

In the Bible's account of creation, as we have seen, the universality of God's concern is clearly established. Moving on further, we come to what is certainly the central event of the history of the people of God – their election. God chooses a particular people in a specific context to be the vehicle through which his purposes are to be accomplished. This particularity is the key to understanding not only mission but also the role of the people of God in this mission. If we separate God's universality from his particularity, we allow for the removal of uniqueness from the Christian mission as the focus shifts away from the church and its role in God's mission. The danger of identifying universality with universalism also arises. These errors are counteracted when we hold together God's universal concern for all his creation and his particular concern for the people he has chosen.

Israel, the vehicle of God's blessings

The first sign of God's intention to work through a particular group is revealed in his choice of Abraham, through whom his mission is to be accomplished. Abraham receives a glimpse of God's ultimate purposes. God declares that he is going to bless many people through his descendants. God, who is universal in his lordship, chose a particular man to accomplish his universal purpose. But even at that point God makes it clear that his particularity is not to be confused with exclusivism. God's mission has always been accomplished through individuals, and this has been evident throughout the history of his dealings with mankind. But the reason he has always chosen one individual is so that others can receive God's blessings through that individual. Election confers no exclusive right to the riches of God, but rather the privilege of being the vehicle of blessing for many. Israel's deepest struggle was to accept that God had intended the nation to be a vehicle for, not the sole possessor of, his salvation.

The fact that God's particularity implies no exclusive claim is the fact with which Jonah was to struggle later. A superficial approach to the book of Jonah fails to see that the prophet is really a picture of Israel in her refusal to accept that God's purposes ultimately included even the so-called heathen nations. Jonah had no problem in accepting that judgment could be pronounced on Nineveh, but to offer grace was another matter. The picture is one of an exclusivism which hindered God's mission.

Israel had to be reminded repeatedly that God had chosen Israel only as the channel for his blessings for the world – as the beginning of the wider purposes that he was eventually to reveal. Lesslie Newbigin states:

> From the beginning of the Bible to its end we are presented with the story of a universal purpose carried out through a continuous series of particular choices. God, according to the biblical

picture, although he is creator, ruler, sustainer and judge of all people, does not accomplish his purpose of blessing for all peoples by means of a revelation simultaneously and equally available to all. He chooses one to be the bearer of his blessing for the many.[6]

A comparison of the doctrine of election with the Hindu teaching of individuality helps to bring out an aspect of the biblical message urgently relevant to mankind today. The Hindu teaching of individuality is that 'the ultimate reality is identical with the true self ... which is the eternal subject, pure consciousness, pure spirit'.[7] Newbigin points to the danger of this belief that individuals require neither other persons nor a created world in order to achieve their true destiny. The Bible, in contrast, points to individuals existing only in relationship with other persons and as part of the created world. 'Interpersonal relatedness belongs to the very being of God.'[8]

Newbigin goes on to affirm that there can be no salvation except in relatedness. This kind of stress is needed to counter both the existentialism of westerners and the independent spirituality of the East. Neither can exclusivism be justified. Israel was elected so that through her privilege all others could become related to one another and to God. A chosen individual was responsible for a body. Election meant that salvation, demonstrated through the initiative of God in one people, was to be passed on to other peoples. Salvation must be made available to others, and no-one can receive salvation in isolation from others. Election must be viewed in the context of human interrelatedness. We can therefore question the teaching that the Holy Spirit works apart from the community that God is building, or that it is possible to be an 'anonymous Christian' – saved by Jesus Christ even while professing another faith.

Israel, a people with a mission

God was in no way bound to choose any particular people. From a human point of view, neither Abraham nor Israel was an ideal choice. But God chooses in his sovereignty. Abraham was to 'leave' and to 'go' (Gn. 12:1). God called a particular people, not restricting his ultimate purposes to this group but clearly declaring that all the peoples on earth would be blessed through Abraham and his descendants. This people was to be only a vehicle, and that was itself a privilege. Israel was constantly reminded that this privilege brought with it a greater responsibility involving the salvation of the nations (Gn. 26:4; 28:14; Is. 42:6–7; 49:3–6). The particularity of election established the universality of God's purposes.

Israel was a people with a mission, a light to the nations, a particular people with a universal purpose. God said of his servant, 'I will put my Spirit on him and he will bring justice to the nations' (Is. 42:1). This servant would act in faithfulness (v. 3), and through his obedience offspring and descendants would also enjoy this blessing (44:3). Despite Israel's faithlessness and stubbornness, the Servant was chosen and through him the splendour of God was to be displayed (49:3). The sharpened sword and the polished arrow will bring the salvation of the Lord to the ends of the earth (49:2, 6). God's mission is universal.

The servant signifies what God wanted Israel to be. But because Israel failed, God chose a servant who was rejected by his fellows yet accepted by God, who suffered yet would be glorified, who was isolated yet who was the one through whom God's salvation would be made available to many. Israel was meant to be the people who would faithfully fulfil God's mission to the world. They failed, but God chose his servant to fulfil this task. God's purposes for humanity would ultimately be fulfilled despite human disobedience and unworthiness, since God's mission is ultimately God's responsibility.

Israel failed to recognize God's wider purposes. They even failed to recognize the significance of God's love for them. In Hebrew, election implied a free choice from among several alternatives. God did not have to choose Israel. The whole world was at the disposal of the sovereign Lord who had created it, but he chose to concentrate his love on a people through whom the world would receive the redemptive benefits of God's mission.

The 'servant' concept is one of a variety of biblical images that bring out the richness of God's redemptive purposes. The servant of the Lord in Isaiah is one whom God chose (41:8–9; 42:1; 43:10; 44:1–2; 45:4). The term is also frequently applied to Moses and to David, chosen by God to perform specific tasks for him. A servant is one who carries out his master's mission. The Servant Songs in Isaiah highlight God's missionary purposes, and are key passages for understanding election and its relation to mission. In the light of their fulfilment in Jesus Christ, we can see that his followers are now the vehicle by which God will communicate his message to the world.

Another rich image which brings out similar themes is that of the marriage union in Isaiah, Jeremiah, Ezekiel and Hosea (Is. 54:4–8; 62:4–5; Je. 2 – 3; Ezk. 16; 23; Ho. *passim*). Israel belonged to God as a wife to her husband. Yet he had taken possession of her not only for his own pleasure but in order to fulfil his purposes. The marriage would be fruitful; sons and daughters would follow.

God's mission is not stagnant and static but fruitful and dynamic. This fruitfulness comes out even more clearly in the imagery of the vineyard in Hosea (2:15) and Isaiah (5:1–7). As the owner of the vineyard expects his vine to bear fruit, so God expects from his people a purposeful fruitfulness. Israel, God's possession, was often rebuked for her faithlessness to God who had called her in order to accomplish his missionary purpose through her.

Jesus Christ himself made use of this vine symbolism, identifying himself as 'the true vine' (Jn. 15:1–7). The significance for God's mission is clear. The failure of Israel to fulfil its God-given mission compels God to act decisively. Jesus Christ now embodies that mission. His disciples, the church, are now to fulfil God's ultimate purposes for his world. The church stands today in Israel's place in God's mission. Even though the church fails, the Bible does not indicate that this mission will be taken away from her. The last phase of God's plans is to be accomplished through Jesus Christ, the true vine, and the church which he has commissioned. This corrective is necessary to check the tendency to see the world rather than the church as the vehicle of God's mission. The concept of Israel's election is a forceful factor in the argument.

An expression of God's love

The fundamental event of election must be considered within the framework of God's covenant with Israel. The covenant clarifies the conditions of the bond that is brought into being by God's choice of Israel. Neither election nor the covenant, however, can be understood apart from God's love, in which they are rooted. Jeremiah stresses this: 'I have loved you with an everlasting love; I have drawn you with loving-kindness' (31:3). Israel's religion expressed the fact that God had chosen her to be his own, to be fully committed to unfolding his purposes to the world around them. God chose Abraham, bringing him out from Ur into the promised land of Canaan. God's promises to Abraham concerned everlasting purposes beyond the narrow confines of a single clan. He was to be a blessing to the whole earth.

The fact of election, even where it is not explicitly stated, is the underlying theme of the entire Old Testament. Yahweh's sovereignty and activity are universal, yet his choice of a people to fulfil his plan is particular. Israel could not take this favour for granted, and God was constantly to remind her that she did not deserve it. Deuteronomy 7:6–8; 9:4–6 remind us that she was not attractive, numerous or righteous, but weak, small, insignificant and unattractive. God's love would not be limited to Israel; her privilege was to bring unlimited blessings to all nations. When Israel failed, God in his sovereignty called even a pagan ruler, Cyrus, to fulfil these purposes. This privilege was eventually to be given over to the people of God in the widest sense, the church.

This fact establishes the centrality of the church in the fulfilment of God's purposes. God is not raising up a new people today with no regard for what he did in history. So there is no room for ideas of salvation outside the purposes of God revealed through his people and recorded in the Bible. Since the church is the chosen vehicle of God's mission to the world today, it is the God–church–world sequence, rather than the God–world–church sequence, that gives us a biblical basis for mission.

Covenant

Earlier we spoke of three horizons that should compose our perspective on mission: the revelation of God in the past, recorded in the Bible; the future culmination of the kingdom; and the present in which we find ourselves.

These three horizons are linked most cohesively in the theme of the covenant. It is the one Old Testament theme that provides a continuing, all-inclusive horizon for God's dealings with humanity. So essential is the doctrine to understand God's relationship to humanity and the world that some have sought to develop the idea of history alongside the acts of the promise-keeping God. We shall discuss this in the next chapter, but for the present I propose to draw out some implications of this covenant relationship between God and mankind.

Throughout the Old Testament the covenant-making God is revealed. The covenant is implied even in God's promise to Adam in Genesis 3:15. Although the word is not used in this passage, and there is no sign of the distinctive elements of the covenant to be made later between God and human beings, it does contain the important promise from which commentators draw out a reference to the redemption to be made available in Jesus Christ. Fallen as they are, and in need of the redemptive work of God's grace, the man and the woman can antici-pate the unfolding of God's purposes, implied in this promise of triumph over Satan and sin. This act, which would one day be revealed in Jesus Christ, would apply to all the offspring of Adam and Eve.

Universality and eternity

The first explicit reference to the covenant appears in God's dealings with Noah: 'I will establish my covenant with you' (Gn. 6:18). The note of promise plays a key role. Here is an aspect of God's mission we often forget. Our mission today is not something new, that bears no relation reference to history. God, in his intimate concern for mankind, wants to fulfil his purposes on the basis of an agreement he has already made.

An examination of the covenant with Noah reveals two others aspects relevant to mission – universality and timelessness. These were to be emphasized later in God's covenants with Abraham and David. Genesis 9:16 explicitly refers to the everlasting covenant between God and all living creatures on the earth. Further, this covenant, as a covenant between God and the earth itself (Gn. 9:13), indicates that his redemptive purposes involve all of the created order. We have often held a restricted, individualized idea of salvation, and this is not wrong provided it is seen in the context of God's covenantal concern for all of creation. The more we study passages such as these, the more we discover how narrow our view of mission has been. God's concern is as wide as his kingdom, as we see when we consider his mission in the light of his concern for his entire creation.

Unfortunately, we have sacrificed the Hebrew understanding of wholeness in favour of a Greek or Hindu dualism. The dualism of the spiritual and the material, the body and the soul, has stifled our thinking and hence mission today. There is of course a distinction between the material and spiritual, but we should not see a dichotomy in what God intended to be a unity. Moreover, even if we have accepted that the human being is one whole, we have tended to think of God as interested only in humanity. If

God is truly Lord of all the created order, then his concern must extend to all creation as well. Because the covenants relate to the whole of creation, we should adopt a more positive attitude to it. Only then shall we be able to develop a fuller understanding of God's mission.

It is in Abraham that we most clearly see the width and extent of God's mission. The covenant God made with Abraham in Genesis 15 and 17 is not separate from the rest of his dealings with mankind. Abraham was just as a much a sinner as Adam, but God chose him in order to demonstrate his purposes for the whole world. Abraham was to be the vehicle through whom nations were to be blessed. God's ultimate concern was the redemption of a people he would form for himself, and it is through this people that he would accomplish his plans for all of his world. In this sense, Abraham was to become the father of nations.

In his covenant with David, God promised: 'I will make the nations your inheritance, the ends of the earth your possession' (Ps. 2:8). There are elements here of the covenants with both Adam and Abraham. Certain aspects of these promises were undoubtedly fulfilled in the immediate future. However, when we consider the messianic promise in Psalm 110:4, 'You are a priest for ever,' we can see that as well as an immediate fulfilment it has an eternal significance. God's mission to humanity has a timelessness about it, and hence John can refer to Jesus Christ as 'the Lamb that was slain from the creation of the world' (Rev. 13:8). In a sense, then, it is presumptuous on our part to claim to be exploring the depths of God's mission. Since we want the horizon of our present to interact with the horizons of the biblical past and future, however, we must be open to having our horizons continually expanded.

Salvation universally available

Concerned for the salvation of the world, God singled out a man, Abraham, through whom the nations were to be blessed. Paul pleaded with the Jews to understand that God's blessings applied not only to Abraham's physical descendants, but that the Gentiles too would be incorporated into the 'family' of Abraham. Abraham was called not only so that he would become the father of a great nation but also so that through him 'all the families of the earth would be blessed' (Gn. 12:2–3). Abraham's fatherhood, like God's promises, extends to all who believe, even Gentile nations. Through the fulfilling of these promises in Christ, God was to form one universal family through Abraham. The heart of the promise to Abraham is the availability of salvation for all, and through his obedience, the exciting prospect of God's mission was revealed.

This thrilling fact causes the psalmist to call peoples to sing to the Lord. 'Declare his glory among the nations, his marvellous deeds among all peoples' (Ps. 96:3). Even families of nations are called to ascribe to the Lord the glory due to his name (Ps. 96:7–8). This same emphasis is found in the prophets, particularly in Isaiah 40 – 55. If Israel had faithfully accepted the mission given her by God himself, she could have powerfully fulfilled the divine purposes. In his sovereign plan, however, God had determined to fulfil them in Jesus Christ. Paul, in a mixture of excitement at the glorious gospel and frustration at Israel's failure, reasons that 'because of their transgression, salvation has come to the Gentiles to make Israel envious' (Rom. 11:11). This envy, he hopes, will bring about their salvation.

The covenant fulfilled in Jesus Christ

The continuity of the Davidic covenant and its fulfilment in Jesus Christ give God's mission a complete perspective which any treatment that makes no reference to the Old Testament would lack. In speaking of the throne that will last for ever (Ps. 45:6), God looks ahead to the reign of Christ and to the culmination of all the covenantal promises in him. Although these promises had already been partially fulfilled in the geographical and numerical growth of Israel, there is an even greater significance to

God's covenant. The promise to David takes the promise to Abraham even further, from the immediate fulfilment into eternity. This is no new covenant distinct from the older covenants. Rather, in the Davidic covenant the older covenants were renewed and extended to reveal God's final purposes for his people. As we stand in the fulfilment of God's covenant in Jesus Christ, we stand in the fullest revelation of God's mission.

The implications of this covenant are explicitly and implicitly woven into the New Testament passages that point to the fulfilment of the messianic psalms (2 and 110) in Jesus Christ. The significance of the Davidic covenant for God's missionary purposes as unfolded in the Old Testament is further stressed in Isaiah 55:3: 'I will make an everlasting covenant with you, my faithful love promised to David.' God in his faithfulness would fulfil the promises he had made to his people. In Isaiah we clearly see the widening of Israel's mission and the universality of God's purposes. All nations would be included through God's eternal purposes for his chosen people Israel.

It is only when we grasp the significance of the covenant in the Old Testament that we can see its relevance in the New. Themes in the Old Testament covenants are central to the meaning of the cross and its redemptive significance in mission. The New Testament frequently refers to Jesus' death in terms related to the Old Testament covenants. For instance, the description of Jesus as the paschal lamb refers back to the covenant sacrificial animal: the references to Jesus' blood similarly point to the connection between Jesus' death and the covenant sacrifices. Undoubtedly, then, the covenant is an important area of study for mission today.

Anchoring mission in the covenant of God adds to it a wholeness as well as the inter-relatedness of which we spoke earlier. The church today is integrally linked with God's people in the past, and cannot claim to be a new phenomenon. This continuity helps us to see mission in a fully rounded way, in the context of God's total purposes for his world. The covenant was not for the benefit of one individual or of one élite group but for all of his creation, the people he had formed for his own glory. Israel was constantly reminded that her existence in the world as God's chosen people was not for herself but so that through her all peoples should be blessed.

In fulfilling her mission, Israel would have continued to receive even greater blessings if the inter-relatedness that God intended could have been realized. Israel failed to comprehend this inter-relatedness. This reminds us to see our mission today as being firmly rooted in God's heart and to check any false emphasis against God's Word. Denominationalism and isolationism splinter God's mission into many missions. The whole church must be involved in God's total mission to the world.

A grasp of the extent of God's covenant and of his total purposes for humanity helps us to correct some other restricting factors. We have sometimes over-emphasized the importance of the faithfulness of the church or even of individuals in the fulfilment of God's purposes. We have pleaded with people to accept Jesus Christ, in such a way that the hearer believes that the whole burden for his salvation rests on himself or herself. While in no way disregarding the importance of individual responsibility, we need also to emphasize the faithfulness of the covenant God. Moreover, the stress on strategies and programmes in mission today needs the reminder that God's mission is finally dependent on his firm promise and on his faithfulness. This is not to minimize the part our intelligent involvement plays, but to stress the fact that mission means involvement in God's programme which he will eventually fulfil. If Israel failed, this was to be expected, since she was only a human vehicle. The church today can fail, and undoubtedly has failed, but God in his sovereignty continues to work out his kingdom mission through her. He can use even human unfaithfulness, and in doing so he emphasizes his own faithfulness on which his covenant is based. Mission is ultimately God's prerogative, the unfolding of a plan he has promised to fulfil in order to accomplish his sovereign purposes.

It is in Jesus Christ that we find the three horizons of mission so firmly held together. This comes as a corrective to eschatologies that define the outworking of God's mission as either purely present or purely future. Moreover, an emphasis on the fulfilment of the covenant promises in Jesus Christ does not imply that the church has already received all that is intended in God's plan. The kingdom horizon motivates the church to look forward to a glorious future, but calls its members to demonstrate that they are God's people today. The covenant promises also correct the current over-emphasis on programmatic approaches to mission. God will work out his purposes in accordance with his plans, and neither the church's planning nor the faithfulness of any individual ultimately matters. Remembering the ultimate purposes of God enables the church to appreciate the faithfulness of God as he builds his people today for his kingdom in the future. As we bear in mind the three horizons, we can 'actualize' theology in a way that is essential today. There have been so many individualized interpretations of mission, with a corresponding over-emphasis on gigantic mission strategies, that our task has seemed reduced to a purely human strategy. The church today stands in the same danger as Israel in the past, unless it recognizes that mission is purely God's prerogative. Mission is the outworking of God's plan based on his covenant with the world and demonstrated in his church as she obediently submits to him.

4

God and mission

Mission in any context today brings us face to face with varying and contrasting concepts of God, divine beings and divinity. Because many teachers and teachings have confused millions by their claims, it is important for the Christian to get a grasp of the God of the Bible. There are two factors we will constantly encounter. First, the God of the Bible is a personal God. Not only so; he is, secondly, a personal God who has revealed himself historically. The task of mission is to present this God as clearly and convincingly as possible.

Right from the start we are dealing with contrasting concepts of God. For instance, Hinduism teaches us to accept that all the gods, the devas, are only names and forms of the One Being (Ekam Sat) who himself has no name and no form. When we speak of the biblical God of mission, however, we speak of a God *in* mission. He has personality and can act in history. The fact that a supreme yet personal God revealed himself in historical situations stands in marked contrast to the Hindu claims.

Even the Islamic concept of God, with all the similarities to the biblical God that some claim, confronts us with God's utter transcendence. In spite of Islam's belief that God is everywhere and is to be in the heart of the believer, the idea of his unknowability rules out a personal knowledge of God in the biblical sense.

In relation to such concepts, the biblical doctrine of a personal God stands out as the strong point of Christian mission; it is a mission that relates to people. By and large in Asia and Africa, and now even in the West, we are confronted with impersonal forces as manifestations of God. Buddhism was basically a belief system with no concept of God. Buddha himself did not believe in any special revelation of God, and his teachings are therefore more a philosophy of life than a religion. Only when Buddhism entered China in the first century did radical changes bring about a belief in Buddha as a deity. Buddhism, however, has no teaching of a personal, active God. It is interesting that in the revival of traditional religions some of the gods are portrayed as personal deities.

The recent emergence of the New Age movement builds similarly on the notion of God as a spiritual force rather than as a person whom one encounters. Drawing heavily on Hinduism and Buddhism, the proponents of this movement speak of God in terms of 'being', 'consciousness' and 'essence', without any reference to the historical acts or the personal nature of God. One of the most powerful apostles of the New Age movement, Hollywood actress Shirley MacLaine, claims that she encountered two spirits who taught that God is only a force or divine energy. Even Jesus, she discovered, is only a highly evolved human being.[1]

In the face of such challenges, it is imperative to learn about the biblical God, particularly in relation to his personal nature and historical acts. Even within the church itself, there have been calls to redefine our understanding of God in more active, dynamic terms. Having considered some trends in mission, we shall now examine some of the attributes of God that demonstrate his identification with humanity in all its joys and struggles. We shall discover a God whose very essence is the basis for mission today. Mission begins with God himself, not merely because he is the God of mission but because his very character is mission. Since we have not sufficiently explored mission from this perspective, we shall attempt to draw out some implications for mission from the very personality of the biblical God. Such a study will be significant in our quest for a theology of mission for today.

God is holy

God's activity in history reveals his holiness (Is. 6:3; Ezk. 20:41; 28:22, 25). When God redeemed Israel from her bondage in Egypt, and amid their jubilation, Moses and the 'sons of Israel' were reminded that he is 'majestic in holiness' (Ex. 15:11). The basic distinction between God and mankind is God's holiness. When human beings come face to face with God's holiness they are convicted of their utter unholiness. Isaiah, for instance, confesses: 'I am ruined! For I am a man of unclean lips, and I live among a people of unclean lips' (Is. 6:5).

God, who desires his people to be a holy people, is on a mission to bring them back into a holy relationship with himself. The biblical understanding of God's holiness is not static, as though holiness were something God wanted to keep for himself. It is, rather, something he desires to impart to his people. The dynamic, personal nature of the holy God arouses in human beings fear, reverence and a consciousness of their own unholiness. In his grace he makes Israel holy, separating her for his purposes, and imparting to her a holiness that stems not from herself but from her relationship to God. That is Israel's motivation to continue to seek God's holiness: 'Be holy because I, the LORD your God, am holy' (Lv. 19:2).

One significant fact must be noted. In popular terms, holiness is seen very much as the responsibility of the individual in search of fellowship with God. The individual spares no effort, even seeking total separation from the material world and chastising himself mercilessly in order to attain nearness to God. In the biblical sense, however, holiness is acquired not through self-effort but wholly through the grace that God bestows on his people. 'Holiness is not so much a relation of the creature to the creator as of the creator to the creature.'[2]

Holiness is God's divine prerogative, but it is something he longs to share with those who trust in him. Essentially, then, God's mission is to impart his holiness to sinful creatures. If people could become holy by their own efforts, they would have no need of God's mission or even of God. This ought to be our thrust when we communicate the message. There is no way in which one can become holy except by receiving the holiness that God imparts through Jesus Christ. Mission, then, must be seen in the light of God's desire to restore his creation to the holy relationship with him which he had originally intended. This holiness is entirely God's but can freely be ours.

In its fullest sense, 'holiness' refers to more than moral attitudes and carries an eschatological significance. It is thus a vital aspect of the goal of God's mission.[3] God in his holiness not only desires all creation to become holy, but also convicts the world of sinfulness and unholiness. The Old Testament prophets cried out against Israel's unholy rebellion against God's demands and pointed constantly to God's holiness. Because God, in creating his universe, desired it to become holy, sin will not ultimately prosper. God's holiness ensures that his universe will ultimately be restored to perfection. A new heaven and a new earth are the goal of God's mission, and in his holiness he desires that his creatures, who will dwell with him in this restored universe, should become holy (Rev. 21; 2 Pet. 3:13). The concept of holiness thus becomes highly significant in the development of a theology of mission, promising the restoration of the holy relationship between the creator and his creation.

God is angry

God's holiness is inseparably linked with his wrath. We must grasp this in order to refute unfounded criticisms of the biblical understanding of the anger of God. The problem arises when we begin to speak about holiness and wrath as individual and distinct characteristics of God. Seen separately, they seem incompatible, just as anger and love seem incompatible. But when we hold them together we can reconcile any apparent conflict. When we are faced with the question 'How can a loving God be an angry God?' the answer must be, 'Because he is a holy God.'

Some think that while the God of the Old Testament is a God of wrath, in the New Testament we encounter a God of love. The temptation to draw a dichotomy between the God of the Old Testament and the God of the New must be rejected from the start. Wrath and love are characteristics that make God a personal God. Wrath 'is a personal quality without which God would cease to be fully righteous and his love would degenerate into sentimentality'.[4] If mission involves confronting human sinfulness, there is no reason to deny that God demonstrates his wrath against that sinfulness. In fact, it is only when we see God's love in the context of his wrath that we can appreciate the true impact of the grace of this loving God. Scripture depicts this wrath plainly. Various terms in the Old Testament bring out the intensity of God's reaction to sin.

The Hebrew *'ap̄*, 'to be angry', intensified to *ḥᵃrôn 'ap̄*, 'to burn with anger', expresses the fierceness of his anger. The terms *ḥēmâ* (anger), *'ᵉḇrâ* (rage), *qāṣap̄l* (to [be]come angry) and *zā'am* (to address angrily, to curse) are utilized to characterize God's wrath. 'There is intensity in the terms themselves and in the construction in which they occur to convey the notions of hot displeasure, fiery indignation, and holy vengeance.'[5]

Some offer strong arguments against this understanding of the biblical God. Only pagan gods, it is maintained, are depicted in such 'capricious' and 'vindictive' terms. The biblical God does not inflict punishment on his worshippers. Irritational passion has no place in the character of the God of the Bible. It is on these grounds that the idea of propitiation was rejected by C. H. Dodd and B. F. Westcott.

In a masterly treatment of this problem,[6] Leon Morris agrees with Dodd and Westcott that we should reject any idea of God's wrath that likens it to the rages of the pagan deities. But he concludes that the fact of God's wrath cannot be eradicated from the Old Testament.

It is not the monopoly of one or two writers, but pervades the entire corpus so that there is no important section of which it could be said, 'Here the wrath of God is unknown!' . . . the concept may need to be understood carefully, but it is so much part and parcel of the Old Testament that, if we ignore it, we cannot possibly enter into a proper appreciation of the Hebrew view of God or of man.[7]

If we are to proclaim the righteousness of God and his just demands, it is the wrath of God that will underline the seriousness of humanity's condition. God cannot tolerate sin, and his longing to save mankind from sin is based on both his love for mankind and his wrath against sin. As Morris points out,

If we think of an uncontrollable outburst of passion, then we have a pagan conception, completely inapplicable to the God of the Old Testament. But if we think of a wrath which is the reverse side of holy love, a flame which sears but purifies, then we have a conception which is valuable not only for an understanding of the ancient Scriptures, but also for any right conception of the nature of God.[8]

Our proclamation of the gospel, as we fulfil God's mission, cannot avoid mention of God's anger at humanity's sinful condition. The most popular 'gospel message' today is easily the one that glosses over God's wrath and emphasizes his love. God's wrath is his reaction against humanity's sin, so when we preach the gospel we must address human sin. If sin is truly what the Bible says it is – opposition to God – God must react against it, and his wrath is that reaction. When we hold together all the characteristics of a holy and loving God, there should be no problem in accepting his anger as an integral part of his nature. When the message of the Bible is preached in its entirety, and the Holy Spirit convicts people of their sinful condition, the totality of God's nature is being expressed.

God is jealous

In the pluralistic environment that is becoming the religious climate all over the world, we increasingly need to proclaim the God of the Bible over against the gods of the other religions. Dialogue is helpful, but only in so far as it makes us aware of the situation we confront. For the Old Testament believer in God, there was hardly any room for attempts to come closer to adherents of other faiths. Any compromise was rejected. In revealing the Decalogue to Moses, for instance, God refers to himself as a jealous God (Ex. 20:5). The idea of God's jealousy may face the same criticisms as the concept of God's wrath. So we must understand this aspect of God's nature correctly. Jealousy is that aspect of God which causes him to claim Israel's total commitment in a personal and exclusive bond, like that between husband and wife. God will not share his people with any other so-called gods.

As with God's wrath, God's jealousy cannot be understood in isolation from other characteristics of God's relationship with his people. The concept of jealousy must be seen as an expression of God's intense love for his people, linked with his covenant with Israel. God, as sovereign initiator of the covenant, desires his people to maintain the covenant bond in order that they may enjoy its benefits. Partners within a marriage bond, in demanding exclusive love of each other, display a similar attitude. Undoubtedly, the problem of God's jealousy arises when it is understood purely in terms of a selfish, human expression of the emotion. Within the covenant bond, however, it is a necessary expression of the character of God who claimed Israel's exclusive loyalty. His jealousy is another pointer to his personal nature. Surrounded by concepts of divine activity as an all-pervasive, impersonal force, the biblical teaching about God's jealousy forcefully underlines his personal longing for an uncompromising and intimate relationship with his people. What a contrast this is to the Hindu understanding of the Supreme Being who lacks all involvement with and concern about his creatures! This Being has no covenantal obligations to fulfil, nor does he feel any compassion that would compel him into a redemptive response involving a sacrificial relationship with his people.

Within the covenant relationship, the people of Israel were under obligation to serve the Lord with all their heart, with all their soul and with all their might. But God too was under an obligation to maintain this bond he had initiated. In this context his jealousy is integrally linked with his desire that Israel would faithfully fulfil the demands of this bond. Israel, being weak and surrounded by powerful pagan influences, could easily surrender her affection to the gods whose images seemed more attractive than the image-less Yahweh. Just as Israel faced the challenge of seemingly more powerful religions, we too can be threatened by the growing influence of other religions, and in such a situation it may be easy to seek compromises that would ensure security amid growing antagonism.

God did not settle for a relationship of compromise with Israel. It had to be all or nothing! In fact, this passionate exclusivism was responsible, later in Israel's history, for the recovery of the conviction of God as sovereign over all the universe.[9] God's dominion, although revealed to and manifested in Israel, was really over all life, history and the entire universe. And it will ultimately be revealed to all mankind. The heart of mission reveals the heart of God. He wants all creation to be exclusively his, and so jealous (or zealous) is this desire that he provides for the salvation of all men and women even though it means a temporary severance from his own Son. Love and compassion become inseparable from jealousy and exclusiveness, and God's mission demonstrates his burning passion for his people.

God is loving

Having dealt with wrath and jealousy, we must move on to God's love, lest our discussion seem too negative. The Bible richly depicts the love of God through the covenantal relationship he establishes with his people. The Hebrew word *ḥeseḏ* is best translated 'covenant love',[10] referring primarily to the steadfastness of the unfailing love he pledged to Israel. This love is directly linked with the covenant and conditional upon its very existence. That is assumed throughout the Old Testament.

The loyalty and faithfulness involved in this covenant love have implications for both parties to the covenant. In the Old Testament, however, the burden rests wholly on God to maintain his faithfulness despite Israel's unfaithfulness. This is powerfully depicted in Hosea's commitment to his unfaithful wife, Gomer, an allegory of the relationship between God and Israel. Because of his own attitude to his unlovable wife, Hosea was able passionately to proclaim God's steadfast commitment to Israel, a commitment that would fulfil all the obligations of the covenant he had made with his people. Hosea was addressing God's people at a time when their apostasy had reached a climax after a prolonged period of backsliding and rebellion. It is at such a time that God reveals once again his covenant love, graphically pointing to the pathetic condition they had reached.

But against this background the covenant love of God is accentuated. It is a love that recoils from meting out punishment, a love that is willing to forgive, a love that would cause the wayward wife to listen once more. Hosea remembers the work of God in the exodus (Ho. 12:13), when Israel, although she could in no way have demanded deliverance, had nevertheless experienced God's mercy and love. The same God (Ho. 13:4) and the same hope (Ho. 14:4) would issue in God's love ultimately working out his purposes for his wayward people. Assyria would not save Israel. It would be God's unfailing love that would eventually restore life and vitality to his covenant people (Ho. 14).

Hosea was looking beyond Israel's temporary humilitation to their exaltation when the wider purposes of God would be fulfilled through the incarnation and cross of the Lord Jesus Christ.

God's mission without his love would be no mission at all. It is this covenant love that strengthens our mission in the world today, giving it the dimension of a tangible relationship over against the experiences being offered by religions adapted to the mood of today's commercialized world. In contrast, the love of God proclaimed in mission is not a novel, emotional response to the present-day longing for love. God's covenant love for Israel was a picture of his love for the whole world. The book of Jonah depicts a people who appropriated God's love for themselves alone. Nineveh had rejected God, and human thinking would suggest that God should therefore reject Nineveh. But God's covenant love, the love that compels us into mission today, is a love that in his eternal purposes he has constantly demonstrated to all who will believe in him.

This leads us to another, equally significant, Old Testament word for love, *'āhēḇ*, which we can translate as 'personal love'. In contrast to covenant love, this love is not limited by covenant conditions, but expresses the personal will and nature of the lover. *'Āhēḇ*, in fact, expresses the personal nature of God's love as he seeks to demonstrate his concern for people he has made in his own image. Once again, the motive behind this love is not necessarily that love is offered in return, or even that those receiving this love are lovable in themselves.

We have already considered God's election of Israel and noted that God did not choose Israel because of anything in her but only because of his divine love. This comes through clearly in Deuteronomy 9:4–5, where Israel is reminded not to think that God would give them the land because of their own righteousness or integrity, and in Deuteronomy 7:7–8, where God says he chose them not because they were a large number of people worthy of such love. He chose them for his own sake, out of his own desire, unfaithful and unlovable as they were.

The significance of this for mission is clear. God saves not just the attractive, the mighty, the educated and the intelligent. He desires all people, regardless of their attitudes to God, to be brought into the relationship they have been created to possess. The history of mission is full of accounts of missionaries going to the fiercest of peoples, the 'ugliest' of human beings, to demonstrate this love. *Ḥeseḏ* and *'āhēḇ* combine to give mission a passion that originates in the very heart of God. Missionaries go, not only because they are convinced that God has chosen in his sovereign will to save all who will believe in him, but also because God's love is demonstrated in the urge to sacrifice comfort and familiar surroundings in order to go into difficult and even hostile situations. Such is the love that has characterized the western missionary era of the recent past. In numerous cases it has been a recognition of this love that has led to conversions to Christ. Mission without love is an empty programme without God's passion.

God is righteous

The Hebrew word for 'righteousness' is derived from a root meaning 'straightness', and is to be understood within the context of a relationship. There are certain demands that need to be fulfilled to maintain the rightness of a relationship, and the result is the demonstration of straightness or rightness. God's righteousness is a fulfilment of his relationship with mankind – he deals with mankind on the basis of the obligation he has laid upon himself to act rightly. Hence his call for the righteousness of his people is a call to respond to the righteousness that God himself demonstrates.

Righteousness, then, is fundamentally the fulfilment of the demands of a relationship that God has initiated. Every individual has numerous relationships, and each of these involve the individual in fulfilling certain demands. The demands will naturally vary from relationship to relationship. 'Righteousness' means 'right relationships'. God as a righteous God is true to his character when he seeks to establish a right relationship with his people.

There is, however, a danger that we may settle for an understanding of righteousness only as a status into which we are brought. But righteousness 'is an action much more than a state'.[11] Because of the demands laid on him, a 'righteous' person must act justly. The prophets constantly require God's people to practise justice. Righteousness is not a quality or a state to be acquired only so that a right relationship with God may be enjoyed. The emphasis is rather on the fact that this relationship must be expressed in concrete acts that demonstrate and strengthen right relationships with God and others. Right and just relationships are the focus of the message of the prophets.

Recent calls to Christians to consider social justice, no matter how one-sided, have served a useful purpose in shaking us out of our privatized piety into showing concrete concern in keeping with the righteousness of God's kingdom. The Old Testament clearly outlines the justice within relationships that Israel was to maintain and uphold. The prophets attacked their failure to do so on the ground that social injustice violated the very righteousness of God on which Israel's just relationships were to be built.

The Jubilee principle of Leviticus 25 and Deuteronomy 15 is commonly quoted in discussions on the theme of justice. This Mosaic exposition of social justice involved protecting the rights of those under bondage. This kind of justice, it is argued, became the central feature of the ministry of Jesus. If this is accepted, then it is of utmost importance to our mission that we look carefully at the role of justice.

There is a close link between the terms 'justice' and 'righteousness', and the Old Testament calls our attention to the fact that their implications also are interlinked. The over-emphasis on 'justice' purely in the sense of fairness and equality in social relationships is therefore questionable. On the other hand, we have already seen that justice is not to be defined wholly in terms of a 'spiritual' relationship either. The question then arises: what is the best way of approaching the issue, particularly in the context of fervent challenges to consider evangelism as involvement in struggles for justice?

The thrust of the prophetic challenge is that while the people of God readily wanted to enjoy all the privileges of the covenant, they were unwilling to express their responsibilities in actions that reflected this relationship. Despite our evangelical attempts to ignore the call to justice in the present-day mission context, it is clear that God expects his people to demonstrate just relationships which will in turn bring about just structures in our world. There is no doubt that the prophets were ultimately concerned about Israel's spiritual condition, but their spiritual condition was manifest in their perverse social condition. Mission cannot be preoccupied with the vertical relationship alone, even though this is the primary relationship. A righteous vertical relationship is demonstrated in righteous horizontal relationships.

The Jubilee, seen in this context, becomes a powerful reminder to Israel of the ultimate relationships that we are to expect in the kingdom of God. The deprivation of rights of the poor and the oppressed, the improper distribution of wealth, the prevalent greed and materialism, are social evils which have pervaded mankind as a result of sin. Kingdom people must begin to live out kingdom relationships here and now, and this was central to Jesus' message.

Further, we should carefully consider the context within which the prophets cried out for justice. Those who were challenged to live out God's righteousness are those who had already entered into a righteous relationship with God. We cannot demand social righteousness without first calling people to a right relationship with God. The one-sided stress on social justice without an adequate stress on people's relationship with God is untenable. It is premature to press for right relationships in the world today without first presenting the God of these right relationships. The over-emphasis on social justice in mission must be challenged in the light of the context in which prophetic calls for justice were made. The prophets' cry for justice came in the context of a theocratic people. God's justice and righteousness are known through the people who accept his kingship and not through those who reject or even remain indifferent to it. The primary thrust of mission, then, is to present the God of justice rather than to emphasize the justice of God.

In our great concern for justice and righteousness we tend to forget that they will finally be brought about by God, not by us. His messianic mission will restore the wrongs in his world, and righteousness distinguish his messianic rule. One of the terms applied to the Messiah is 'my righteous servant' (Is. 53:11). He is the one who will ultimately demonstrate God's righteousness. Yet this does not exempt the church as God's people from demonstrating messianic justice here and now. The church must be the model and the agent of God's right relationships in the world today, because the Lord of the church is the Lord of righteousness.

The suffering God

We have recently been reminded that purely academic theology, being no more than cold formulations about God, was unable to meet the needs of the struggling masses of humanity. Where theology was not merely academic, it was all too often an individualistic mysticism. Most of the time, it is true, we have hesitated to relate the cross to the harsh realities of our world. Much of the theological tradition of the early church betrayed a Greek influence with its doctrine of God's impassibility. The Latin *impassibilis*, meaning incapable of suffering, was used of God who, being transcendent, was thought to be beyond humiliation and suffering. Actually, this was more in keeping with Plato's argument that the gods were beyond pleasure and pain, or even with Aristotle's 'Unmoved Mover', than with the God of the Bible. If God could feel pain, it was argued, how could he be omnipotent and immutable?

Hindus, too, firmly believe that the Brahman is bliss and therefore beyond suffering and without the capacity to share in the sufferings of humanity. Further, the idea of karma stands as an obstacle to understanding the suffering of God in his redemptive sacrifice. Since suffering is regarded purely as the result of previous evils, God could not possibly suffer.

A well-known Asian response to the theology of impassibility came in the theology of pain propounded by the Japanese scholar Kazoh Kitamori.[12] He wrote of the pain of God that heals our pains, developed from Jeremiah 31:20 where God speaks of his heart yearning for Ephraim. About the same time, Dietrich Bonhoeffer wrote that 'Christ helps us, not by virtue of his omnipotence, but by virtue of his weakness and suffering'.[13] One must be careful, as Jürgen Moltmann reminds us, not to over-emphasize suffering, since 'the mysticism of suffering can easily be perverted into a justification of suffering itself'.[14] Yet this need not excuse a retreat into academic or individualistic interpretations of the cross and suffering.

The world today is more ready to respond to the call of a God who hurts in our sufferings than to one who forgives sins. There is so much confusion over personal sin that people see no need to reflect upon their sinful condition. By contrast, suffering in all its variety is something we can all understand and respond to. The Bible depicts a God who cares.

As we search the Old Testament in order to learn about the suffering God, we encounter anthropomorphisms which we may want to dismiss as purely figures of speech. But to place God beyond pleasure and pain is to depict a God who is less than the God the Bible portrays. God is a God of suffering, who not only understands but feels pain. This is the God who will truly address our world of sin and suffering today.

Although many attempts to speak of the God who suffers miss the mark, we must accept the challenge and look afresh at the Bible. Charles Ohlrich[15] helpfully draws our attention to the need for a theocentric understanding of the

Old Testament. We have frequently spoken of God's justice, goodness and wisdom, but we have not properly recognized God's pathos. For instance, says Ohlrich, when we look at passages recording God's concern for humanity's waywardness, we concentrate on what they say to us without seeking to understand what they reveal about God's heart. Take Ezekiel's allegory of unfaithful Israel. God says to her: 'You trusted in your beauty and used your fame to become a prostitute. You lavished your favours on anyone who passed by and your beauty became his' (Ezk. 16:15).

In *The Suffering God*, Ohlrich observes that

> When we hear God speak of his people this way, many of us react by examining our own lives to see any ways in which we might be living as a prostitute in God's eyes. We turn inward and become introspective because God sounds angry. We read the passage egocentrically, taking it as a revelation about our sinful lives. This is not entirely wrong ... But we need to cultivate a God-centred consciousness that would take in the full meaning of the passage. Failure to understand the passage theocentrically is to miss half the meaning.[16]

As we accept this pointed reminder, we must admit we had missed the force of God's words. One wonders whether the viewpoint we need to develop could more appropriately be termed a 'theocardiac' viewpoint, one that attempts to see things from the perspective of God's heart. For it is only when we rightly perceive God's passionate heart that we will capture the force of his concern for mankind.

Missiology from the standpoint of God's kingdom must restore a holistic theology in which the heart of God is seen to involve not only love and justice but also agony and suffering. This theocardiac view of the Bible will open up more of God's heart, so that we recognize the intensity of God's pain when he called to Adam, 'Where are you?' (Gn. 3:9). We shall see this not as an academic inquiry but as a cry of despair, because his plans for the glory of mankind had been thwarted by their rebellion. From then on God's heart of suffering, like that of a father pitying his children, continually seeks people out in order to save them.

In conclusion, in our enthusiasm to present the personal nature of the God who works in our historical situation, let us not be trapped into commercializing our presentation to meet the needs of the world. God is working and reconciling the world to himself in order to conform us to his image. We must present the 'bigness' of our God. Both the Islamic and the Hindu ideas of the Supreme Being are a challenge that we need to consider. Our gospel preaching has often accommodated God to the whims and fancies of the people to whom we have preached, calling them to accept or reject Jesus Christ. When we consider the greatness of the biblical God, we should rather ask, 'Who am I to accept or reject God?' It is this kind of God that the world awaits.

5

Promise, history and mission

We have already stated that two unique characteristics of the God of the Bible are his personal nature and his historical revelation. Having considered some of the personal attributes of this God of mission, we now turn to some aspects of his activity in history. No-one who reads the Old Testament can doubt that it was written in the context of a people's history. The mission of God is worked out in history, and it is in establishing this historical revelation of this God that we ground mission in the real world. Throughout their history, the people of God see him act in concrete situations, manifesting his redemptive purposes for the world.

The revelation of God in history

The credibility of the biblical mission leans heavily on the fact of God's relationship with humankind and their world. One attempt to maintain the historicity of God's revelation came from the German theologian Wolfhart Pannenberg, who argued that it is within a universal, historical perspective that the reality of God's revelation and the historicity of the resurrection can be maintained.[1]

Pannenberg boldly declared his intention to assert that God revealed himself through his acts within history. This sequence of acts was not to be seen as a segment of history, nor was any single event to be regarded as distinct from the rest of history, or as existential or supernatural. Pannenberg first refuted two important views that were prevalent. On the one hand, Rudolph Bultmann had dissolved history into 'the historicity of existence'. On the other, Martin Kahler's 'redemptive history' spoke of the content of faith as being 'supra-historical'. Both these positions stemmed from the same theological motive: the desire to substantiate faith within the prevailing attitude towards history. It was generally accepted that critical-historical investigation left no room for redemptive events. Therefore, the theology of redemptive history took refuge in the idea of supra-history or even prehistory, while the theology of existence settled for security in the 'historicity of the individual'. Recognizing the inadequacies of these two attitudes to revelation and real history, Pannenberg saw his task as pressing home the fact that redemptive history can be demonstrated to have taken place within an actual historical framework.

Pannenberg points out that because the God of history has manifested himself through his actual historical acts, we can talk about his revelation within history. When the theology of Rudolph Bultmann held sway, this was a revolutionary proposition, since the Bible and revelation had been subjected to devastating attacks. The German theologians popularly known as the 'Pannenberg group' went on to make a major contribution in their book *Revelation as History*. The group dared to claim that God's revelation was historical at a time when it was embarrassing even to speak of God in history.

The problem that had faced many scholars was the Kantian assertion that revelation could not be objectively grounded. Pannenberg deliberately sought to break away from this assumption, though he cautiously stated that 'the self-revelation of God in the biblical witness is not of a direct type in the sense of a theophany, but is indirect and brought about by means of the historical acts of God.'[2] Accepting Barth's concept of God's self-revelation, Pannenberg was keen to use this concept theologically to show that God revealed himself within his historical acts.

It is instructive to note what Pannenberg means when he says that God's revelation is not direct but indirect. If God were to reveal himself directly, the content of this revelation would be solely God himself. By contrast, an indirect communication initially involves some content other than that which is to be communicated. Thus, when God reveals himself indirectly, we do not initially receive God as the immediate content. Rather, we receive the historical acts of God which indirectly express something about God. Ultimately their purpose is to reveal God, although not directly or immediately.

This seems reasonable, although a serious problem could arise if Pannenberg were to suggest that even Jesus is not the direct revelation of God. He attempts to avoid such a conclusion, however. In his desire to substantiate his claims in a way that the historian will find reasonable, Pannenberg proposes a theory based on the fact of the resurrection. 'If Jesus having been raised from the dead is ascended to God and if thereby the end of the world has begun, then God is ultimately revealed in Jesus.'[3] Pannenberg is saying that only at the end can God be revealed in his divinity. Because in Jesus' resurrection the end has already begun, therefore, God has revealed himself in Jesus. 'Only because the end of the world is already present in Jesus' resurrection is God himself revealed in him.'[4]

We may still have a problem with this, but we must commend Pannenberg's effort to blend the theologian's confidence in the biblical revelation of God and in Jesus' resurrection with a commitment to history in the observable, factual sense. He also blends a commitment to life in the present with a commitment to the future fulfilment of God's promises. Mission grounded in history alone would be merely a human effort with no ultimate dimension to motivate it. An absolute commitment to a future actualization, however, compels us to a creative proclamation and demonstration of the gospel of the kingdom which reveal God's purposes within our history. It is this blend of the present and the future that constitutes the essence of a truly biblical yet historical mission.

Pannenberg's thesis, based on the climax of God's historical revelation in the resurrection of Jesus Christ, carries an important corollary. He goes on to point out that 'the transition to the Gentile mission is motivated by the eschatological resurrection of Jesus as resurrection of the crucified one'.[5] Old Testament prophecy had looked forward to the self-demonstration of God as an event that would take place before the eyes of all peoples, who would then recognize the exclusive divinity of Israel's God.

> A Gentile mission seems to have arisen for the first time as a result of the conviction that the resurrected Jesus has now already been exalted to Lordship in heaven and consequently the news of his Lordship is to be carried to all nations.[6]

The mission of the church, already being exercised in this climatic phase in history, thus becomes urgent as God empowers us to proclaim to everyone the good news of the coming kingdom.

Israel's historical consciousness

It is because of her interest in actual history that Israel stands apart from her neighbours. This is not to say that there was no concept of history in the nations surrounding Israel. But the uniqueness of Israel's historical consciousness lies in her belief in a God who acts within actual rather than mythical history. The ancient Orient could not see how history, full of continual changes, could provide meaning to life. So they could not see how their gods could work in actual history. To protect their concept of divine beings, they chose to believe in divine events outside time and space. God could not be part of real history, as that would threaten his existence.

Moreover, Israel saw history as moving in a linear fashion, purposefully, towards a goal. In marked contrast, the concept of history outside Israel was cyclical. As history moves on in its linear fashion, the biblical God constantly breaks in to initiate new events that fit within a sequence moving towards the ultimate fulfilment of his plans. This linear concept helps us to develop a holistic view of history, and within this whole the individual events that God initiates find their meaning. This view gives meaning to mission as a historical manifestation of God's ultimate purposes for the redemption of mankind and of his world.

In developing an understanding of this linear movement of history in relation to God's dealings with mankind, Pannenberg links God's promises and their fulfilment within that movement. In an early essay he stated that 'within the reality characterized by the constantly creative work of God, history arises because God makes promises and fulfils these promises.'[7] For instance, in Deuteronomy 7:8–9 we read that 'it was because the LORD loved you and kept the oath he swore to your forefathers that he brought you out with a mighty hand and redeemed you from the land of slavery . . . Know therefore that the LORD your God is God: he is the faithful God, keeping his covenant . . .' Yahweh, having established a covenant with Israel, and being faithful to it, will fulfil his promises to his people. History is the tension between his promises and their fulfilment.

Moreover, Israel was gradually given a perspective that embraces the whole of history. By the time of David, God's promises are seen to span a period that reaches beyond the limitations of immediate time. David was told that he would build God's house and that God would establish the throne of his kingdom for ever. Israel not only had a conception of God working in a particular sphere of reality, but saw this sphere as a part of a total perspective held together by God. History is a total reality that moves in a line towards a God-purposed goal. It is only when we grasp the importance of this total perspective that we are able to grasp the whole meaning of God's mission.

Because of the continuity of God's redemptive purposes for humanity, mission, as we perceive it from the accounts of God's revelation, forms a continuity within history. The transition from the Old Testament to the New is smooth. In fact, we can understand the significance of Jesus' mission only within this total perspective of God's dealings with mankind. As Pannenberg says:

It is of great theological significance that the confession of Israel and that of the community of the New Covenant consistently hold fast to the one history of God which binds them together. The connection between the Old and the New Testament is made understandable only by the consciousness of the one history which binds together the eschatological community of Jesus Christ and ancient Israel by means of the bracket of promises and fulfilment. Jesus is the revelation of God only in the light of the Old Testament promises.[8]

Understanding the whole of history

God's mission is a whole mission and must therefore be understood from within the perspective of the whole. Attempts to define mission from within particular contexts or even within a particular time will not fully accord with God's mission. The concept of promise and fulfilment, in keeping with God's covenant, gives us this holistic perspective and enables us to see the sequential, historical involvement of a personal God as he unfolds his mission to mankind. This concrete view of mission is what we need to establish within the completeness of God's redemptive process for both mankind and its world.

The conviction of God's control over all of history was most fully developed in the apocalyptic literature. Both within and outside the biblical context there is not only a belief in God's lordship over all of history but also an expectation that his kingdom would suddenly break through to reveal these eternal purposes to the world. The mission of God was not seen as reaching only a particular people. God's lordship over all the earth meant that his plans must embrace all the earth. So strong was this conviction around the time of Jesus that some scholars view him as an apocalyptic seer who proclaimed the kingdom message.

The apocalyptic literature demonstrates the continuity

between the Old and the New Testaments. It is heavily characterized by an eschatological viewpoint. Theologians have forcefully drawn attention to the neglect of this theme, particularly since Ernst Käsemann's essay 'The Beginnings of Christian Theology'.[9] Käsemann reminded us that, rather than making apocalyptic the final chapter of our dogmatics, we should make it the first.

In the light of the revival of the apocalyptic theme in recent decades and its restoration to its rightful place in theology, studies have stressed the eschatological orientation of Old Testament historical consciousness. This emphasis inspired Pannenberg to revive the universal apocalyptic interpretation of history. This perspective asserts that there is no conflict between the present and the future. God is working out his purpose within a whole, and this gives meaning to the present. Within this whole, the future gives meaning to every contemporary experience. Such an eschatological dimension to mission will assist in widening the scope of our concerns as we participate in God's purposes for his world.

Although we speak of the future impacting the present, we are not referring to some supra-historical dimension. That would raise the same problems as were experienced in trying to reconcile the concrete involvement of God with existential ideas of history.

We need to restore the biblical stress on historicity as a valid corrective to the devaluation of history in the religions of this world. The fact of creation in the past, and the movement of God's purposes towards the new creation in the future, show that history is moving purposefully towards a goal, in contrast to the cyclical view of the traditional religions and today's purely present understanding of history. Such misrepresentations eventually spell meaninglessness.

Mission is not about the entrance of an individual, or even of a people, into the kingdom. It is about the coninuity of the community of God who fulfils his purposes in historical events, in real space and time. Accepting that God's kingdom purposes are worked out in concrete historical reality avoids the spiritualization of mission.

Even the ethical understanding of the kingdom espoused from Kant to Ritschl in the nineteenth century failed to grasp this historical significance. God's kingdom cannot be discussed apart from its concrete manifestation in history and in the present. When we see the kingdom as existing only in human hearts, or when we remove it into the security of the future, we fail to do justice to the biblical reality of the kingdom. The Bible speaks of a history in which the past and the present move meaningfully towards a future. It gives us a glimpse of this future goal towards which history is moving. Mission today, then, must take seriously both history and eschatology.

The note of promise and fulfilment in God's purposeful acts in history brings hope to a world lost in despair and hopelessness. Biblical mission is a mission of hope, and we must project this as clearly as possible, not merely to win larger numbers but in order fully to depict the impact of God's mission for the world today. A fresh understanding of history will also infuse meaning into an otherwise meaningless world of shattering events. It is this hope of a concrete future that compels the church to creative action towards the fulfilment of God's kingdom.

Yahweh, the covenant name

As we study the Old Testament from the perspective of God's promises within actual history, we do well to start with a brief study of the character of God as denoted by his name Yahweh. He is the covenant-keeping God, continually fulfilling the promises he made to his people. God revealed himself to Moses in the name I AM WHO I AM, which could also be translated I WILL BE WHAT I WILL BE (Ex. 3:14). In distinction to the gods that Moses had been familiar with through his knowledge of other nations, God would prove himself unique. He would personally manifest himself through fulfilling promises he had made, and would reaffirm to Israel that he is a God who remembers. In Hebrew thought, to remember is to act, so Yahweh is depicted as one who 'repeats his acts of saving grace towards his people Israel again and again, and in this way fulfils his promises, and shows his self-consistency'.[10]

To the Hebrew, to know God's name was to know his character. The name was far more than an identity label. Israel has no need to design its own God in ignorance, for God had revealed himself as one who was active in the history of his people. God is concerned for his people, and so enters into their history, freshly revealing his nature to them.

His disclosure of his name is integral to and inseparable from the history of Israel, in which he constantly reveals himself and reminds his people that he rescued them from bondage (*e.g.* Ex. 20:2; Ezk. 20:5; Hos. 11:1; 12:9; Am. 2:10; 3:1–2). These reminders not only call Israel back to her first love but also assure her that God would fulfil the promises he made to his people as he dealt with them in their history. The mission of God is integrally bound to the fulfilment of these promises. On the ground of a historical relationship with their God, Israel's faith represented a radically new kind of response to divine reality. Their confidence was in a personal God who had revealed himself to people in history and in a covenant which would ultimately be fulfilled in God's kingdom. This covenant, however, would constantly make an impact on their present mission – in fact, on their history.

A deeper study of the implications of God's name will draw attention to the reality of this covenant relationship in terms of the fulfilment of God's promises.[11] For instance, to render the name as 'I cause to be what comes into existence' bears reference to God's dynamic lordship over all creation and to the fact that historical happenings have their origin in his sovereign will. What greater reminder did Israel need than to know that their God, the controller of history, would work history out to fulfil his purposes?

A theology of mission must pay attention to this characteristic of God as promise-fulfilling, and to its relevance to our history. The fall took place in history and God has provided salvation within history. A missiology grounded in history will not hesitate to express itself in concrete, historical demonstrations of God's concern for his world. Human history is integrally tied in to God's working in the world. And if this is so, God's mission influences every aspect of human history. The all-embracing nature of God's lordship must be demonstrated in an all-embracing mission to the world.

Promise in the Psalms

The theme of promise is the underlying emphasis throughout the history of God's people as they anticipated the fulfilment of his declared intentions. A cursory glance at the Psalms would clearly bear this out. In relation to the mission of God, we shall find the messianic psalms, in particular, a worthwhile study.

The promises given to the patriarchs and to Moses will find their fulfilment in the Messiah, who will draw people to the imminence of their ultimate fulfilment. Psalm 2, for instance, underlines the universal significance of the messianic mission, which, fulfilled in Christ, points to the extent of his authority. God's dominion extends over all the kings of this earth, who are warned to take heed. To Israel this is certainly a note of hope. Despite the uproar of the nations around, despite all their devising of vain plans and the rulers who take counsel together, their God is in control and he will give Israel the nations of the earth as their inheritance.

The fact that God is Lord does not mean that everyone accepts that lordship. In fact, the contrary may be true. Ultimately, however, his kingdom will be established and his sovereign reign will be experienced. Any view of history which fails to look beyond the present will only leave the church in utter despair. Its mission will be defeated right from the start. Conversely, triumphalistic attitudes to mission centring on success-oriented strategies in the present cannot be justified either. A complete understanding of God's mission, derived from a biblical view of history, will see defeat as well as success as part of the ongoing life of the people of God. The sovereign God, in his concern for the whole, has a purpose in every event that forms part of his dealings with humanity.

Several other psalms make bold and emphatic reference to the fulfilment of the purposes of God through the mission of the coming king. Some of these references are used by the writer to the Hebrews to show how Jesus Christ fulfils those purposes (Heb. 1:5, 8–9, 13; 2:6–8, 12; 5:5–6; 6:17, 21; 10:5–7). David's kingship foreshadowed the final revelation of God's lordship which would crown the mission of his people. Through the ministry of Jesus, God asserted that he was still the promise-keeping God. His eternal throne, and the universality of his lordship, are now demonstrated in Jesus Christ and his death and resurrection. The mission in which he calls his disciples to be involved is the mission that was already envisaged in God's plan and inaugurated in the life and longings of his people.

We catch a glimpse of the goal of God's mission in Psalm 87, where we see Israel's struggle to accept God's universal concern for all people coming to an end. The privileges of citizenship in Zion are now extended to Rahab, Babylon, Philistia, Tyre and Cush. Israel's self-centredness restricted her vision of God's mission as being concerned merely with herself. God certainly dealt with other people, but only, the nation believed, in judgment. But the goal of God's mission is the availability of salvation for all. The boundaries of the people of God will stretch beyond Israel. Zion is now, figuratively, the dwelling-place for all who trust God. The content of our proclamation and the goal of God's mission are this glorious coming together of all who will put their trust in God. For this reason the psalmist exhorts us to proclaim to the nations the glorious purposes of God: 'Tell his glory among the nations, his marvellous deeds among all peoples' (Ps. 96:3).

Promise and the prophets

Against the background of this understanding of the whole of history, and of the fulfilment of God's promises in the unfolding of his mission, the role of the prophets is significant. In highlighting the purposes of God in faithfulness to his covenant people, the prophets emphasized this same promise-fulfilment framework that we have been considering. God's word to his people through his messengers was all of a piece with the rest of his dealings with them. The prophets reminded the people about God's purposes for mankind. On the basis of the covenant made in the past, they called the people back to a relationship with God in the present. The prophets draw upon the whole of the people's history to substantiate the mission of God. Within this perspective, the prophets proclaim the historical truths of the ongoing kingdom mission. In no way can we, 'prophets' in today's mission, attempt to do anything different.

As we approach the ministry of the prophets in the light of God's mission, we discover a continuing emphasis on God's promises and their fulfilment. The eschatological expression 'the day of the Lord' signifying the day when God would finally demonstrate his sovereign control, is a passionate element in the prophets' message. God would show his purposes and vindicate his people. God's mission, however, also implies judgment for Israel.[12] This in no way violated his love, but because Israel had strayed from the covenant with her God she needed to be sternly reminded of his plans. God would judge sin, but would triumphantly usher in the future that had been promised to his people in all his dealings with them throughout their history.

In announcing Israel's judgment, the prophets announced God's wider purposes which would bring about the fulfilment of his kingdom. Amos, for instance, scathingly attacked Israel with no assurance of hope for them in the day of the Lord (5:18–20). They had been delivered from Egypt and promised redemption, but that was no guarantee of their salvation and their place in the kingdom of God. Any unfaithfulness in the form of a lack of concern for goodness and justice was to be condemned. Those who sought good, hated evil and established justice would enjoy the grace of God (5:14–15). This faithful remnant formed the link between the promises of God and their fulfilment in Jesus Christ.

In Micah, too, we see how the fulfilment of the Old Testament prophecies points forward to the universal lordship of Jesus Christ. In the context of a stern and condemnatory proclamation, Israel is reminded of her origins in God (6:4–5). The purposes for which they were saved would be fulfilled on the grounds of the covenant promises (7:20). This hope, however, should result in justice, mercy, and all else that was synonymous with God's nature (6:8).

Micah was realistic, for he knew what people undergo in times of defeat and despair. He reminded Israel that, despite the physical destruction of Jerusalem and the temporary cessation of prophecy (3:6–7), the purposes of God would have universal application (4:1–5), and peoples would stream to the Lord's temple. This centripetal attraction of God's house is directly linked with the expectation of the Messiah (5:2–5a). His greatness would reach to the ends of the earth (5:4), bringing to pass promises which he gave 'to our forefathers in days long ago' (7:20).

Malachi is the prophet chronologically closest to the New Testament. He reminded Israel of God's love for them, going back to the patriarch Jacob (1:2–5). He announced the coming day of the Lord with the declaration that a Messenger would come to prepare the way and to make the offerings of Judah and Jerusalem pleasing to the Lord (3:1–4). References to the Mosaic covenant (4:4) and to the return of Elijah (4:5) point to God's earlier promises, and to their fulfilment amid judgment. Those who 'feared the LORD and honoured his name' (3:16) would enjoy the privilege of being God's treasured possession (3:17).

In the light of even this brief study, it is surprising that so little attention has been paid to what the Old Testament teaches us about mission. The God of mission was active throughout the history of his people, and his people were called to get involved in this mission. God chose Israel to be the channel through which his kingdom purposes would be announced. All his activity among his people clearly pointed to Jesus Christ who would bring the kingdom within the view of his people. The church will continue that mission till his kingdom comes.

Promise and biblical mission today

When we come to mission as depicted in the New Testament and still being carried out today, there need be no doubt about the continued outworking of God's promises. The emphasis is still on the promises of the Old Testament and on their fulfilment in Jesus Christ. God had promised that through Abraham all the families of the earth were to be blessed. The significance of Abraham to God's people is well established in the Bible, and this is the foundational promise that would be fulfilled through Jesus Christ and the mission of the church today.

Although Abraham was only God's vehicle (as the church is today), God in his sovereignty had chosen him to accomplish his purposes for the world. In other words, the emphasis is not on Abraham, but on the promise given to Abraham. The Jews had over-emphasized the man himself. John the Baptist came down scathingly on this belief: 'Do not think you can say to yourselves, "We have Abraham as our father." I tell you that out of these stones God can raise up children for Abraham' (Mt. 3:9). As F. F. Bruce comments, 'Descent from Abraham carried with it no special privilege or merit (even vicarious merit), no special exemption from the wrath to come.'[13]

Both John the Baptist and Jesus (Jn. 8:33–47) clearly state that physical descent from Abraham did not guarantee entrance into the kingdom, and Paul develops this emphatically in this theology. In his letter to the Galatians he underlines the fact that right from the call of Abraham, it is the promise that is central. 'For if the inheritance depends on the law, then it no longer depends on a promise; but God in his grace gave it to Abraham through a promise' (Gal. 3:18). Abraham trusted in the God who had promised the inheritance, and in believing that, he was justified (3:6), Abraham's faith was reckoned to him as righteousness when he committed himself to God, trusting in his word and believing that his promise would be fulfilled.

Paul does not stop with Abraham, for his purpose is to show that through Christ the Gentiles also receive this promised blessing. 'He redeemed us in order that the blessing given to Abraham might come to the Gentiles through Christ Jesus, so that by faith we might receive the promise of the Spirit' (Gal. 3:14). Abraham's offspring now are not merely those who are his descendants in the flesh, but those who are the 'children of promise' (Gal. 4:28). Paul repeats this thought in his letter to the Romans, emphasizing that 'not all who are descended from Israel are Israel' (Rom. 9:6). The promise of God is wide open to all who by faith commit themselves to God through the Lord Jesus Christ.

Jürgen Moltmann, developing the idea of the 'God of the promise', states:

> The promise is no longer exclusive, but becomes inclusive. It becomes universal. The universalizing of the promise comes of its being liberated from the confining grip of the law and election of Israel. If in the power of God, as seen in the raising of the Crucified and, as a result of that, in the justification and calling of the Godless, the promise has become unconditional – of grace and not of the law – then it has also become unrestricted and is therefore valid without distinction.[14]

The 'Christ event', asserts Moltmann, contains the validation of the promise, and through the faithfulness and truth of God the promise is 'made true wholly, unbreakably, for ever and for all'.[15]

We need to underline this universalizing of the gospel in the fulfilment of the promises of God through Jesus Christ. The process takes place, however, within the context of the continuing history that began with God's promise to Abraham and is being fulfilled in Jesus Christ. In a way, there is nothing new about the New Testament. What was anticipated by the faithful in the Old Testament is fulfilled in the New. This overall understanding of history gives meaning to the cross and resurrection and thereby to the ongoing mission of God.

The church in mission stands in line with God's people in mission since the call of Abraham. Just as Israel was chosen to carry out this mission in its time, God has called the church today, within history, to be the vehicle through which his purposes will be accomplished in history. As history moves to its culmination, the urgency of the task before the church increases. No longer can it remain an ingrown, self-centred people. It needs to break out of its barriers – denominational and theological – to be the people that God intends it to be. Its mission is not 'spiritual', in an airy-fairy sense, but is demonstrated in history which is moving towards its culmination in the kingdom of God.

6

The kingdom horizon

We have considered the importance of perceiving God's activity in the whole of history, and of seeing mission as the church's involvement in the fulfilment of God's plans for the kingdom. In the light of the importance of this furthest horizon of God's dealings with humanity, we come now to the controversial theme of the kingdom of God, proposing to draw out come crucial elements that will contribute to a better understanding of our mission. Through a closer study of the implications of the kingdom we shall begin to see how God's plans for the future give present meaning to past revelation. The three horizons must be held together in one interrelated whole.

Some caution is necessary. In the wake of kingdom-of-God theologies that reduced the gospel to humanism, and even more the Marxist programmes of the so-called liberation theologies, evangelicals have hesitated to handle the theme of the kingdom, thereby ignoring what the church and its mission are all about. When we give adequate attention to the kingdom of God, we shall be ready to develop the kind of missiology that will make the gospel real in our context. Reading the Bible afresh, one finds it hard to bypass the centrality of the kingdom in the mission of Jesus.

Rather than retreating once again into an individualized gospel, we need to explore the biblical insights fully in order to reclaim the lost territory of God's reign and to recapture God's widest concern for his people and his creation. A proper assessment of the kingdom and its relation to mission will assist enormously in putting the gospel into practice in a way that reflects this wide concern. As he proclaimed the kingdom, the Lord Jesus became positively involved in every area of human life – spiritual, social, economic and ecological. This rules out any doubt about the range of the gospel of God's kingdom.

Jesus preached the good news of the kingdom of God and provoked his hearers, the Jews, to extend their idea of it way beyond the merely nationalistic boundaries to which they restricted it. In a similar way today, reminders of the kingdom of God challenge us to break out of the narrow limits we have set for God's reign. When we see mission in the light of the kingdom we realize how narrow we are when we insist that all that God is concerned about is people's spiritual salvation. The kingdom horizon shatters all our limitations, compelling us to appreciate the full wealth of God's desires for the world.

The gospel of the kingdom, far from being merely a spiritual manifestation of God's mission, has very material effects. It is said that the principal factor that saved Britain from a catastrophe like the French Revolution was the revival which God used John Wesley to bring about. The concrete dimensions of the gospel have always been there for us to appropriate. In the religious environment of Asia, where there is usually no concrete link between the spiritual and the material, the biblical gospel will need to be *demonstrated* if it is to be accepted as the truly viable alternative to the traditional religions that are currently gaining fresh ground.

The kingdom of God in Jesus' message

To Jesus, the kingdom of God was of prime concern. Mark records how Jesus proclaimed the good news of the kingdom at the commencement of his ministry (Mk. 1:14–15). It is clear that Jesus was talking about a reign rather than a realm. He was already pointing to the future as he announced his lordship. To speak of God's future reign, however, does not mean that it has no implications for the here and now.

God's reign has often been seen as pertaining to the church alone. This position has in fact denied God's lordship over everything, even when our words have asserted otherwise. If God is Lord of all, his lordship must be made real throughout the world today. Lesslie Newbigin reminds us that in speaking of the kingdom of God,

> we are not talking about one sector of human affairs, one aspect of human life, one strand out of the whole fabric of world history; we are talking about the reign and about the sovereignty of God over all that is, and therefore we are talking about the origin, meaning, and end of the universe and of all man's history within the history of the universe.[1]

He goes on to conclude that 'the reign of God is his reign over all things.'[2]

Even the disciples were unclear about the kingdom. Jesus had to deal with a nationalistic misunderstanding in the disciples' minds at the time of the ascension. 'It is not for you to know the times or dates the Father has set by his own authority' (Acts 1:7). The rebuke was necessary because despite Jesus' intensive teaching over three years they had failed to grasp the complexities of the kingdom (which we too struggle to decipher). We can draw out some inferences to assist us in our discussion.[3]

First, the kingdom of God is opposed to the kingdoms of this world. It is absolutely miraculous, depending on God, and hence we cannot hasten it by our own efforts. Confident that God will work out his plans, we are to await the coming of his kingdom patiently. This is implied in the parables of the mustard seed (Mt. 13:31–32; Mk. 4:30–32) and the yeast (Mt. 13:33). This leads some to avoid social action, claiming that we are not to be involved in the kingdoms of this world. We ought, however, to interpret this teaching in the light of the rest of Jesus' teaching on the kingdom before reaching such a conclusion.

Second, God's kingdom will come in a cosmic catastrophe ushered in by the appearance of the Son of Man

(Lk. 17:26–35; Mk. 13:24–26; 14:62). Jesus thus aligned himself, not with the concept of an earthly, nationalistic messiah, but with the expectation in the Jewish apocalyptic tradition of the Son of Man. At the same time he avoided describing future events in detail, although he clearly used apocalyptic imagery (*e.g.*, the heavenly feast in the kingdom of God, Mk. 14:25; Mt. 8:11). Connected with this toning down of apocalyptic ideas is Jesus' rejection of all attempts to discern signs of the end: 'You cannot tell by observation when the kingdom of God comes. You cannot say, "Look, here it is," or "There it is!"' (Lk. 17:20–21, REB). The warning comes to well-meaning biblicists who will strain at the text to work out precise details of the second coming. And yet, Jesus himself does give us some signs for our own intelligent discernment.

Third, although Jesus shared with the apocalyptic witness a cosmic, universal eschatology rather than a political, nationalistic kind, he upholds the belief that the primary purpose of God's plan was to reach the world through Israel. It was not his intention to conflict with Old Testament teaching in any way. As we have seen earlier, however, this does not mean that Israel had a special claim to God's grace, but that she was to be the vehicle by which God's purposes would be demonstrated to the world. Her unfaithfulness would be severely judged, and this is why Jesus reveals that Israel will be put to shame by the heathen on the day of judgment (Mt. 12:42; Lk. 11:31), and that the kingdom would be taken away from them and given to the Gentiles (Mt. 21:43).

Fourth, we cannot enter into this kingdom without obedience to Jesus (Mt. 7:24–27), and a willingness to sacrifice to the point of being hated by one's family (Mt. 10:21–22, 37). There is no automatic entry into the kingdom, as implied in universalistic claims about God's desire to save everyone regardless of their commitment. We enter the kingdom on the basis of our willingness to surrender everything in order to receive God's great gift (Mt. 13:44–46). Although entry into this kingdom in the fullest sense lies in the future (Mt. 25:34; Mk. 9:43–47), the kingdom is already present in the person of Jesus. To be committed to Jesus, then, is to experience his kingdom.

Finally, the kingdom of God is a transcendent and a supernatural realm which God brings to us from above. We experience the kingdom in Jesus himself. In him the future kingdom becomes present, having already appeared in his words and deeds. The distinctive element in Jesus' teaching on the kingdom is that the kingdom of God is inseparable from his own person. The evangelistic message of salvation through Jesus Christ becomes an offer of the person of Jesus himself. Salvation is not a feeling or an event but a very real relationship. Our message must emphasize this fact. God in Jesus Christ embraces the believer in a relationship that brings the future reality of the kingdom right into the present.

The kingdom of God in the person of Jesus

We have noted that Jesus' person is inseparable from the kingdom. This fact needs further exploration, since it will shed light on the present dimension of the kingdom. For instance, in Jesus' assertion that 'if I drive out demons by the finger of God, then the kingdom of God has come to you' (Lk. 11:20), Jesus' power over Satan demonstrates the present power of God's kingdom.

This means that the benefits of the authority of the kingdom are available to believers even now through the presence of our Lord Jesus. The kingdom mission in Asia and Africa still manifests Jesus' authority over satanic forces. Perhaps, in our attempts to accommodate the gospel in the modern technological environment, we have been guilty of our own kind of 'demythologization'. Some, particularly those trained in the West, find it hard to accept the reality of the demon world and dismiss it as mere superstition. Yet the realities we confront have much to do with demonic manifestations. The confrontation is a kingdom confrontation.

Further, Jesus refers to his presence as the presence of the kingdom. Luke records Jesus' reply to the Pharisees' question about when the kingdom of God would come: 'The kingdom of God is among you' (Lk. 17:20, REB, NIV mg.). The translation 'within you' in some versions is misleading. Although it suits the personalized Christianity that we evangelicals have fashioned for ourselves, God and his kingdom are not to be tailored to human misconceptions.

The God who will appeal to Asia and elsewhere is the God who is big enough for people to enter into rather than the other way round. A kingdom vision will dispel any powerlessness we impose on Jesus Christ and his demands. Howard Marshall points out that 'Jesus speaks of men entering the kingdom and not the kingdom entering men.'[4] Since Jesus' presence is the presence of the kingdom, we can correctly see Luke 17:20 as meaning that the kingdom is within our reach or even within our grasp. We have no need to look around for the kingdom of God, for Jesus points out that it is present where he himself is present.

That is why Jesus assures those who acknowledge him before others now, in this world, that he will acknowledge them before the Father in heaven (Mt. 10:32). Not everyone who says 'Lord, Lord,' will enter this kingdom, but only those who obediently do 'the will of my Father who is in heaven' (Mt. 7:21). To those who respond to Jesus' words and put them into practice, the future rule of God becomes a reality here and now in the words and deeds of the person of Jesus and his followers. With the emphasis on the fact that Jesus himself represents the kingdom, it becomes clear that the kingdom refers to God's reign and authority demonstrated through Jesus' followers. It is a kingdom of people committed to God's reign and authority who work to make it real in our world today in anticipation of its ultimate realization. Everything, whether open demonic activity or the material and secularistic ideologies that stand against God's message, must be confronted by the claims of the kingdom through the mission of the kingdom's citizens here and now.

Again, in placing the emphasis on God's reign, we need

to be careful not to exclude the idea of a territory. I am not saying that we should claim geographical territories here and now. But if we ignore God's rule over the earth now, we will have problems accepting his rule over all of heaven and earth in the future. As we have already discussed, God's creation, now groaning for redemption, will again be totally under God's authority.

The kingdom present and future

One complex aspect of the kingdom in Jesus' preaching is his reference to it as both present and future. Although he draws a distinction between these aspects, he blends them into one and the same message quite frequently. This is clear, for instance, in his parables in Matthew 13, where his hearers find it hard to understand the kingdom as both present and future. Although the seeds of the kingdom appear insignificant and small now, its influence will be all-embracing and powerful when it grows into its fulness.

While there is no doubt that Jesus speaks of a present reality, complications arise when we try to reconcile this with a future kingdom. In his discourse on the last days, Jesus clearly indicates events to follow in the future (Mt. 24–25; Mk. 13; Lk. 21). Other references to the future concern the Son of Man coming in his kingdom with glory (Mt. 16:27–28) and the kingdom itself coming with power (Mk. 9:1). Another important text occurs in the context of the last supper where Jesus says he will not drink of the fruit of the vine until he drinks it in the kingdom along with his disciples (Mt. 26:29).

The problem has arisen when commentators have tried to interpret each aspect of the kingdom independently of the other. For instance, the liberal theologians of the nineteenth century took the line that the kingdom was purely present, resulting in the 'social gospel' which sought to establish the kingdom in the present world. Conversely, there were those who so over-emphasized the future that there was no room for present application. If Jesus taught that the kingdom had both present and future aspects, we must seek to reconcile these two seemingly conflicting elements.

The kingdom of God was the motif which, interpreted as totally present, determined nineteenth-century theology with its ethical, here-and-now kingdom concern. With the emphasis on our working out of its values within the contemporary world, any reference to the future was eliminated. This assumption was challenged towards the end of the nineteenth century, however, by a thoroughly eschatalogical understanding. Johannes Weiss pointed out that according to the New Testament the kingdom of God would be established by God himself. The future was God's prerogative, not a human doing, or even the climax of the sequence of historical events that led to this kingdom.

The extensive treatment of this subject by Wolfhart Pannenberg assists us in seeing that the biblical emphasis on the wholeness of history is firmly oriented to the future. In Jesus we already have the presence of the future.[5] Rather than retreating into a purely futuristic understanding which bears no reference to the present, we are challenged to reconcile the present and future creatively. We are to underline both the immanence of the kingdom in its impact on life today and the mystery of the kingdom as something to be fully revealed in the future. The kingdom in Jesus' message was neither an other-worldly, idealistic dream nor a totally present reality. Present and future need to be interlinked. And it is in this interdependence of the present and the future that the fullest meaning of the kingdom will be appreciated.

To put it another way, the church and its mission today must draw out of the future the true significance of its being in God. The horizon of the future kingdom influences the horizon of the present to make the church the kingdom community. Building a missiology with the kingdom of God as the central concern forces us into a positive acceptance of the future – a future that does not remain a distant dream but concretely influences the present. Because we are familiar with the way our dreams for the future influence our present, a theology built on the kingdom hope should not be looked upon as a nebulous philosophy.

This means, too, that the identity of the church today is not merely spiritual. It needs to be demonstrated in concrete ways. Unfortunately, a negative understanding of spirituality has led some well-meaning Christians to avoid practical involvement in the world. Taking it for granted that the kingdom was to come in the future, and writing off any who were involved in social action as 'liberals' attempting to build the kingdom here and now, some have retreated into unconcern and non-involvement. This misunderstanding is dispelled when we properly hold together both the present and future aspects of the kingdom. When the church lives out its life in the kingdom horizon, the biblical horizons of past, future and present will truly be brought together.

Most of us have had no problem with various forms of social service that provide education and health care for the needy. But we have hesitated to go beyond this and to see our involvement in the world as the involvement of kingdom people on a kingdom mission. The link between the present and the future must be developed in more concrete ways if we are to see the future tangibly impacting the present. Do we have a problem with desiring a little of the future even now? If our answer is 'no', we must work out the presence of the kingdom in more visible manifestations of Christian witness. Our proclamation of Jesus Christ must begin to make an impact now, or else we are only playing with words.

The dynamic nature of the kingdom

Rather than being problematic, this tension between the present and the future, if developed properly, will reveal the dynamic character of the kingdom. The parables of the kingdom tell us that at present we have only the seeds of the kingdom, which will grow into its full realization in the future. The parables of the mustard seed and the yeast

(Mt. 13:31–33) demonstrate that what is now extremely small will grow and produce change beyond what we can comprehend now. Did not even Jesus' disciples wonder how such insignificant beginnings could culminate in triumph and glory for the kingdom of God?

G. E. Ladd reminds us that

> the kingdom of God is the redemptive reign of God dynamically active to establish his rule among men, and that this kingdom, which will appear as an apocalyptic act at the end of the age, has already come into human history in the person and mission of Jesus to overcome evil, to deliver men from its power and to bring them into the blessings of God's reign. The kingdom of God involves two great moments of fulfilment within history, and consummation at the end of history.[6]

This tension between the present fulfilment and the future consummation is crucial. Those enamoured of Marxist analysis, with its materialistic conception of history, demand an exclusively social, economic and political involvement. Yet if we go to the opposite extreme and become mesmerized by a totally futuristic interpretation of the kingdom, resulting in non-involvement with the material and social dimensions of this world, we can hardly wonder that Christianity is seen as irrelevant. There is a dynamism in the biblical faith which we must express in practical ways in the world, even though this is only an anticipation of the future.

This dynamism clearly emerges in the parables of the mustard seed and the yeast. A small and insignificant thing will grow to astounding proportions and penetrate the whole in the future. The Jews awaited the power and glory of the coming of the kingdom, and hence could not see what was going on when Jesus did not make any great political impact on their society or on their oppressive rulers. How could someone like him inaugurate God's kingdom?

Through the parables, Jesus reminds his hearers that the inauguration of this kingdom is like planting the seed which would produce fruit and mixing in the yeast which would affect the whole lump. In our enthusiasm to influence the present by the future we could fall into the error of making the kingdom purely a matter of our own effort. The mystery of the future must remain till it is revealed. The seeds of the present, however, will continue to grow. Amid the pessimism of the present, the kingdom message must bring hope. Even though Satan rules now, the hidden seed and yeast will grow and consummate the future kingdom in all its power and glory.

This comes as a much-needed reminder in a day when we recognize power only in terms of size and numbers. If the influence of our witness is to be judged by the magnitude of our programmes, the numbers of people brought together, or even the enormous amounts of money invested, we can consider ourselves very successful. We often show off statistics of our achievements to make believe we are being faithful to God's mission. But the smallness of the seed reminds us that it is the quality of the church's efforts that matters most. Recognizing that each church, no matter how small, is responsible for mission in its own locality, will add powerfully to the demonstration of God's kingdom in our world today.

In emphasizing the seed and the yeast, however, we should not imply that Jesus is talking about a natural growth, a gradual unfolding of the kingdom of God. Social-gospel activists view the parables from within a materialistic concept of history in which human effort brings about the future. This runs counter to the mysterious character of the kingdom which, according to biblical teaching, breaks into this world supernaturally. Yet, although God's new age breaks into the old age, the kingdom does extend from this world into the future. Jesus himself told Pontius Pilate: 'My kingdom is not of this world. If it were, my servants would fight to prevent my arrest by the Jews. But now my kingdom is from another place' (Jn. 18:36). The truth lies in the fact that what is available now in Jesus is in essence what will be available in the future when his reign is consummated.

The Lord's supper and the sacraments

As the Passover meal drew to a close, Jesus said to his disciples, 'I tell you, I will not drink of this fruit of the vine from now on until that day when I drink it anew with you in my Father's kingdom' (Mt. 26:29). This important reference to the eschatalogical dimension of the kingdom, linked with Jesus' earlier proclamation of the kingdom as already inaugurated, leads us to further discussion of the theme.

What happened at the table clearly anticipated the fulfilment in the kingdom. The celebration, with its eating and drinking, is not just a symbol of something spiritual in the kingdom. The Old Testament picture of joy in the future is confirmed in the New, represented several times in Jesus' ministry by the enjoyment of a meal (Mt. 8:11; 22:1–14; 25:10; Lk. 13:29; 22:29–30; *etc.*). The communion that is to be part of the church's life in the future was expressed concretely in an essential part of the present life of the kingdom.

Apart from this aspect of celebration, Jesus' words point to something more than merely eating and drinking in the kingdom. Paul writes clearly: 'For the kingdom of God is not a matter of eating and drinking, but of righteousness, peace and joy in the Holy Spirit' (Rom. 14:17). Obviously, Paul is not saying that there will be no eating and drinking in the kingdom, but rebuking the disregard for one another, the lack of true communion, and the absence of kingdom fellowship within the community of believers. The eating and drinking in the kingdom will lack the elements of greed and fleshly craving and instead will demonstrate purposeful participation in common fellowship characterized by righteousness, peace and joy. The kingdom community is to await this harmony in the future, but to make every effort to demonstrate it in the present.

The truth that follows from this is that the Lord's supper is itself a celebration, and not a repetition, of his sacrifice. It is hard to see how some point to the sacrament itself as the sacrifice. Yet the meal does celebrate the fulfilment of this sacrifice. The true significance of the sacrament is highlighted in the fact that the redeemed people of God are commanded to eat and drink in celebration and proclamation of the sacrifice that has brought about their redemption.

It is unnecessary to read into this act any repetition of the sacrificial event. Herman Ridderbos comments:

> Here, the salvation of the kingdom of heaven proclaimed by Jesus' preaching is once again revealed in its messianic foundation and made visible and tangible to his disciples while at the same time being apportioned to them. In one supreme concentration as it were, in one turn of the hand, the Lord's supper focuses the whole of the preaching of the gospel upon Christ's sacrifice and sets the table with it. The disciples are permitted to partake of the bread and wine of this sacrificial offering, and derive from it life and joy as the permanent fruits for the time now to come.[7]

The proclamation of the good news of the things to come stems from the celebration of the firstfruits which we are already tasting. 'For whenever you eat this bread and drink this cup, you proclaim the Lord's death until he comes' (1 Cor. 11:26). We must, then, link the celebration with the proclamation of the good news of Jesus' redemptive work for the world.

The confident celebration of the coming kingdom, and the assurance of the King's presence now, cause the community of the kingdom to rejoice that God's reign has already commenced. Thus the Lord's supper becomes a powerful reminder of the presence of the future kingdom, the anticipation of the glorious future to come. Our three horizons merge tangibly. The covenant community, gathered around this meal in intimate fellowship in the presence of their Master, becomes all that the church should really be. It is the community that awaits the coming of their King. Meanwhile, they live out the kingdom life in the righteousness, peace and joy that demonstrate the very presence of their King here and now.

We should not miss the eschatalogical significance of the meal, or we shall also fail to capture the dynamic nature of the presence of the kingdom. Around the Lord's table, the future becomes the present. Its reality is so tangible that the people of God are sustained and motivated into proclaiming the gospel till the coming of the Lord. The church is unfortunately caught up in an institutional framework that traps it into inaction. The Lord's supper binds the redeemed people of God in a common chorus that cries out in anticipation of the kingdom to come: '*Maranatha!*' But rather than rest in that joy, it is propelled into the mission of the kingdom.

The church and the kingdom

We have recently been reminded of the confusion over the identities of the church and the kingdom. While the ethical understanding of the kingdom stripped this central theme of Jesus of its historical significance, the ecclesiological interpretation causes further damage. The confusion stems from none other than Augustine, who developed the idea that the church is synonymous with the kingdom. We should avoid such a restrictive understanding, and rather draw out more clearly the meaning of the church within the wider context of the kingdom of God.

The primary concern of Jesus Christ in his proclamation of the good news of the kingdom, which is near as well as future, is crucial for the recovery of the essence of the biblical church. The kingdom expresses the totality of God's mission, and the true church must accordingly demonstrate a similar width of concern. It must challenge any tendency of God's people to stand aloof from the world in spiritual exclusivism (regarding the kingdom as solely future). It must also challenge any tendency to accept this world's agenda (as if the kingdom were fully present). The church that stands as a witness to the immanence of the kingdom as well as to its transcendence must discover this reality as it works out the tension between the presence of the kingdom and its future reality. The fact that the kingdom is both present and future gives it its vitality in the here and now, and anchors it in the reality to be revealed in God's time.

The church is not the kingdom

In testifying to this kingdom tension, the church is never to regard itself as the kingdom. It must, rather, discover its role as the people of God who witness to the reality of the kingdom. G. E. Ladd comments:

> If the dynamic concept of the kingdom is correct, it is never to be identified with the church. The kingdom is primarily the dynamic reign or kingly rule of God, and derivatively, the sphere in which the rule is experienced. In biblical idiom, the kingdom is not identified with the subjects. They are the people of God's rule who enter it, live under it, and are governed by it. The kingdom is the rule of God, the church is a society of men.[8]

The church is a people that submits to God's rule and experiences and lives out the kingdom. It is not merely, as Ladd says, 'a society of men', over against the kingdom which is 'the rule of God'. This could be misinterpreted as meaning that the church has no connection with the kingdom. Nevertheless, we should distinguish between the kingdom and the church, defining the identity of each. Yet the relationship between the two is the key to their distinct identities.

The church is not primarily an establishment but the community that represents the kingdom. It is the community of the King or even the community of the kingdom. We must understand this relationship. The community of the King bears the responsibility of testifying to the coming of his kingdom. Thus the present impact of this future kingdom is demonstrated in and through the life and witness of the church. If Jesus' presence signifies the presence of the kingdom, and if it gives life and being to the church, this community called the church is a present demonstration of the future kingdom. All the longings of the faithful in Israel who awaited the fulfilment of God's promises are realized in the church. The church is not the kingdom, but because the kingdom is present she anticipates the total manifestation of the kingdom yet to come. The three horizons converge as the promises of the past and their fulfilment in the future are made real in the present life and witness of the church.

The church, then, lives constantly in the tension between future and present – the tension of being called to demonstrate something it is not. These tensions are resolved as the church submits to Jesus Christ in whom the kingdom is made real. Since Jesus saw himself as the one in whom the kingdom was already being realized, we must demonstrate our anticipation of the kingdom in concrete expressions of the Lord's concern. Jesus did not simply announce the arrival of the kingdom but actually inaugurated it. The church is therefore responsible to demonstrate the actual life of the kingdom, though only in anticipation of its future consummation.[9]

The message and meaning of the kingdom are not to be realized only in the future, but must make an impact on the world today. Our attempts to resolve the tension between what we are and what we are not do not excuse us from being what kingdom people must be. Even those who see the kingdom as wholly future must demonstrate their belief in observable ways in the present. The certainty of the future kingdom must be visibly demonstrated now in tangible expressions of obedience to the King.

The church testifies to the kingdom

The kingdom community, then, although not perfect now, anticipates the perfect community of the future (1 Jn. 3:2). If we take seriously this understanding of the church, we shall be convinced of her responsibility to demonstrate kingdom values even now. In a world of distorted values, the church points to the one who empowers her to live out true values. One of the primary aspects of the church's witness to the kingdom is undoubtedly her ability to live out kingdom values.

We have stressed that the church is not the kingdom, and that the community is not the kingdom. Being the community *of* the kingdom, the people of God exalt the King of their community. Jesus himself never taught the disciples to believe that they were the kingdom. Nevertheless, having taught that he himself represents the kingdom, he now chooses to represent it through the community that acknowledges his kingship. His rule over his people holds them together as the kingdom community. This must be proclaimed and demonstrated.

The mission of the people of God in the New Testament lays heavy stress on both the proclamation and the demonstration of the fulfilment of God's kingdom purposes. The church witnesses to the kingdom in both respects. This twofold character of the church gives it the life and vitality essential to being God's people today. The church as a worshipping and witnessing community must make the truth of the kingdom tangibly accessible to the world. The world must hear the announcement of the kingdom, but it will want to see some concrete demonstration of this message. Consequently the church urgently needs to spell out its kingdom identity, actualizing the message of Jesus through its life and witness.

This is not so say that the church consists of perfect people, able to demonstrate kingdom values perfectly. It is humbling to remind ourselves that it is only by the grace of God that we can claim to have entered into his kingdom fellowship. In his grace we are called, despite ourselves, to demonstrate to the world the ultimate redemptive purpose of God. God's mission is heavily flavoured with his grace. While Paul declares that creation itself groans as it waits for God's redemption (Rom. 8:19–23), here is a people who can already rejoice in having tasted the initial benefits of this ultimate redemption entirely through his grace.

The church's demonstration of the kingdom's mission

This essential link between the church and the kingdom, and the fact that the church stands as a witness to the kingdom, restore to the church its sense of mission. The institutional and denominational view of the church has really stifled a true understanding of both the church and its mission. The church cannot distance itself from mission. The church *is* mission. Mission is not merely an activity related to the kingdom, but is carried out by the church as the community of the King. If the church can rediscover even a fraction of this reality, its kingdom mission will take off.

The church, in its relation to the kingdom, must not only be involved in God's mission but must open the heart of God to the world through its life and witness. The community of the King, as it seeks faithfully to work out its being in God, must express itself in concrete manifestations in a real world, even though the world stands against the purposes of God. All that the church seeks to be, in obedience to its Lord, concerns his kingdom. We have often stripped ourselves of this dynamic by artificially separating our worship within the church and our witness outside. We must integrate the two so that we can discover the inter-relatedness of all facets of life in a powerful demonstration of the kingdom mission.

This life is not just for a chosen few. The proclamation of the kingdom implies its availability to all who hear and are willing to commit themselves to its demands. This kingdom was not to be restricted to one particular race who thought they were the favoured people of God. Rather, Jesus warned the religious leaders that 'the kingdom of God will be taken away from you and given to a people who will produce its fruit' (Mt. 21:43). Israel would no longer be the sole subjects of the kingdom of God, since in his plan many others were now to be included. Jesus taught that before the end comes the gospel, the good news of the kingdom of God, was to be preached to all nations (Mt. 24:14; Mk. 13:10). Gentiles from all over God's world would have the privilege of feasting at the messianic banquet in this kingdom (Mt. 8:11–12).

The Jews could hardly comprehend this fact. The mission about the appearing of the grace of God that brings salvation to all (Tit. 2:11) was as foreign as the Romans. But God addresses this prejudice, breaking down all barriers that restrict the universality of his kingdom mission. We have seen the deep struggle that Jonah faced in his reaction to the mission God gave him. The church today can similarly restrict itself, perhaps not in terms of whom to include in its mission, but by limiting the sphere of influence of the kingdom today.

Mission, then, involves declaring God's purpose to establish his kingdom, and is carried out by a people who in an anticipatory sense make this kingdom real. This suggests that the church must be totally involved in the whole of God's mission. If we are to take the lordship of Christ seriously we must recognize the comprehensive scope of mission in its concern for God's ultimate purposes. The church in its mission today must break out of its own small horizon and discover the implications of God's kingdom horizons. Only then will the reality of the kingdom of God become the dynamic of mission.

Some biblical images of the church

As we read the book of Acts, we can identify some essential elements of the life and witness of the church – worship, fellowship, teaching and witness. We find references to these in the descriptions of the gatherings of the early believers – breaking of bread and prayer, fellowship, the apostles' teaching, ministry and distribution, witness (*e.g.*, Acts 2:42; 4:33, 35; 8:4). These elements could be reduced to two: life within the church itself, and witness outside the church. All that occurs within the church could be described as worship, understood as the submission of the people of God to its Lord and Master; and all that occurs outside the church could be seen as its witness. The true church, then, is the people of God in worship and in witness.

In our attempt to restore the missionary nature of the church, we turn now to some biblical images which place the witness of the church at the heart of its being.

The people of God

We have used the term 'the people of God' frequently, and this is a good image to start with. God assured the people of Israel, 'I will be your God, and you will be my people.'[10] This is the covenant relationship that God would continue with the people of the new covenant. As Peter writes, 'Once you were not a people, but now you are the people of God' (1 Pet. 2:10). This emphasis recurs in Revelation with the thrilling affirmation: 'The dwelling place of God is with men, and he will live with them. They will be his people' (Rev. 21:3).

The Old Testament words *qāhāl* (assembly; usually *ekklēsia* in the Septuagint) and *'ēḏâ* (congregation) refer to the corporate nature of the people of God. In fact, *qāhāl* denotes the gathering of a people in response to God's call (Ex. 35:1; Nu. 16:26). The early church which gathered together in response to God's call would certainly have seen themselves against this background, as God's people.

But God had not called them selfishly to arrogate all his blessings to themselves. God's people are also gathered together to fulfil his purposes.

> See, I have taught you decrees and laws as the
> LORD my God commanded me, so that you may

follow them in the land you are entering to take possession of it. Observe them carefully, for this will show your wisdom and your understanding to the nations, who will hear about all these decrees and say, 'Surely this great nation is a wise and understanding people' (Dt. 4:5–6).

The privilege is accompanied by a responsibility, and these are held together very clearly in these words of Moses.

Peter underlines the same truth when he says, 'But you are a chosen people, a royal priesthood, a holy nation, a people belonging to God, that you may declare the praises of him who called you out of darkness into his wonderful light' (1 Pet. 2:9). The people of God are called to the privilege of worship as well as to the responsibility of witness. Accordingly, if the church really stands on the foundation of the Old Testament revelation, it must see itself as a living community called out by God to worship him as well as to witness to his purposes for the world. The *ekklēsia* is to be seen as a people in motion and not as a static structure. The word 'ecclesiastical' immediately brings to mind denominational and institutional matters rather than the dynamic people which it represents. This living community enjoys all the privileges that God has prepared for it, but longs to reach out and proclaim to the people of this world the blessings that they too can enjoy.

The body of Christ

We come now to the even more familiar New Testament image of the body of Christ. This concept powerfully portrays not only the corporate nature of the community, but also the union between the community and its Lord. Paul uses the concept in various ways. Sometimes he pictures Christ as the whole body and ourselves as members of him (Rom. 12:5; 1 Cor. 10:16–17; 12:27). At other times Christ is the head and his people constitute the rest of the body (Eph. 5:23; Col. 1:18; 2:19). In both cases, however, the lordship of Christ over his people as well as the interdependence of Christ and his people are vividly portrayed.

Here again the stress is on the dynamic nature of the people of God and not on an inanimate structure or organization. It is a community which has the potential to grow, both individually and corporately, into the fulness that God has appointed for it through Christ. But it finds its identity and vitality only in Christ and under his lordship. The power structures of our present-day church, in its denominational and institutional representation of the body of Christ, need to be constantly reminded of the ultimate authority of Christ.

Paul goes on to describe this body, in its several parts, as endowed with a variety of gifts. Some are given for the edification of the body of Christ, while others enable people to proclaim and demonstrate the power of the Lord Jesus Christ. Again we see the church's twofold dynamic. Some gifts equip it to function effectively as a people in worship, while others equip it to witness effectively. The two always go together. Wherever only one aspect of this dynamic is experienced, the church is not fully functioning as God intends.

This challenge must be faced by churches that have become inward-looking, concerned about their own survival. Some seem so preoccupied with their doctrine and the maintenance of the purity of their position that they neglect their outward responsibility towards the world. Equally, some churches are full of fire and action but lack a right concern for their own inner strengthening. The body of Christ is richly endowed with gifts for both its worship and its witness. A truly worshipping church will invariably be a truly witnessing church. The church's double dynamic must be fully appreciated and made real.

God's building

A third image we can consider is that of God's building. The tabernacle and later the temple were central to Israel's worship, and offered a tangible expression of God's presence with his people. But the situation under the new covenant was to be different. When the Samaritan woman raised the question of the temple, Jesus declared that, under the new covenant, people are able to worship God in spirit and in truth. God's dwelling-place is his people, and the new temple of God is to be the redeemed people of God.

Developing our thesis of the church's twofold dynamic, we see first that God depends on his people to house his presence (1 Cor. 3:9–17; Eph. 2:21). The staggering reality is that his people, despite their ingratitude, disobedience and sin, are more important to God than the most stylish structures and exquisite edifices we can erect. This temple is being built up with living stones, namely God's people who are held together in community (1 Pet. 2:5). As they submit to God together, they are strengthened to stand firm on Christ himself as the foundation.

This building, still in the process of completion by the Holy Spirit, is certainly not a building that exists for itself. We are chosen as the building material in order to declare his praises (1 Pet. 2:9). It is carefully constructed to achieve not only perfect architectural harmony inside, but also excellent appearance on the outside. The world marvels at its magnificence, and exclaims in amazement: 'Surely this great nation is a wise and understanding people' (Dt. 4:6).

The church must recover its double dynamic in order urgently to manifest the mission of the kingdom to the world. Unless and until we are able to discover mission in the very essence of the church, all reminders about the missionary mandate will only fall on deaf ears. The task ahead is to explore the true church in its relationship to the kingdom of God and to spell out its responsibility, as the people of God, to witness. The firm location of witness within the essence of the church will lead us increasingly to discover the reality of a church that worships as it lives out its essence as a witnessing people. It is this missionary character of the church, in its witness as God's kingdom people, that needs to be restored.

7

Paul's universal perspective

As we approach the New Testament with our kingdom horizon, we find in its pages a missionary concern just as wide as that which we discovered in our Old Testament studies. It challenges our narrowness. God's concern for his world is unlimited. Any limitations we impose must therefore be broken down in order to accommodate his kingdom plan for the entire world. The New Testament fully expresses how the past and the present horizons are held together by its over-riding concern that the horizon of the kingdom be made real as Christ's lordship over all things is demonstrated.

Interestingly, even the early Christians' vision for God's mission was restricted. Being a predominantly Jewish congregation, they shared the exclusivist attitude of the Old Testament Jews. As God broke this down, we can trace a movement from a Jewish to a worldwide perspective. The people of God had to be continually reminded that God's concern was universal.

Accepting this wider perspective confronts us with an even greater challenge that will extend God's mission to its widest possible bounds – as wide as the lordship of Jesus Christ, whom he has raised 'far above all rule and authority, power and dominion, and every title that can be given, not only in the present age but also in the age to come' (Eph. 1:21). When we consider mission from such a perspective, we cannot limit God's authority and concern to anything less than what God's Word itself outlines.

It is instructive to see the overwhelming influence the future horizon has on Paul's missiology. All the expectations of the people of God throughout their history have been made real in Jesus Christ. The three horizons we described earlier – of the past, the present and the future – become merged into one perspective expressed in the total lordship of Jesus Christ. This is the horizon that the church needs to push itself into accepting. Let us consider the two movements that helped gradually to widen the horizon of the early church to embrace God's kingdom perspective.

The first movement: salvation for all people

Although the early Christians struggled to accept this wide perspective, there is little doubt that the gospel writers had captured the universal dimension of God's concern in the revelation of Jesus Christ. The Christmas message announced peace on earth to people of goodwill. There is no hint that this was for the sole benefit of the Jews. The righteous and devout Simeon confirms the fulfilment of Israel's longings as he joyfully cries:

'For my eyes have seen your salvation,
   which you have prepared in the sight of all people,
a light for revelation to the Gentiles
   and for glory to your people Israel.'

(Lk. 2:30–32)

Luke is clearly concerned not only to write an 'orderly account', having 'carefully investigated everything from the beginning' (1:3), but also to underline as fully as possible the intentions of God in his revelation to mankind. In his two contributions to the New Testament, Luke attempts to depict the movement of mission from a narrow Jewish perspective to a worldwide kingdom perspective. This is the kind of perspective that John the Baptist refers to in the opening pages of Luke's gospel: 'all mankind will see God's salvation' (3:6).

Later, when Jesus announces his mission, all barriers

are broken in the dramatic announcement of his coming to fulfil God's total mission:

'The Spirit of the Lord is on me,
   because he has anointed me
   to preach good news to the poor.
He has sent me to proclaim freedom for the prisoners
   and recovery of sight for the blind,
to release the oppressed,
   to proclaim the year of the Lord's favour.'

(Lk. 4:18–19)

Luke appears to want to emphasize this limitless mission that Jesus has embarked upon – 'a stunning crossing of a social and religious barrier in the patriarchal society of his day'.[1] Conservatives are shocked that tax-collectors, 'sinners', even women, are recipients of the salvific potential of Jesus' mission. 'There is little doubt that Luke sees the connection between this expansive dimension of Jesus and the efforts of the church to move beyond its own frontiers.'[2] Still today the church needs to understand the limitless dimension of mission so that the sovereign control of God is seen to embrace all of his world.

The early church struggled with its Jewish preconception that continued to exclude everyone outside that select community from God's redemption. Had not Jesus made it amply clear that they were to 'make disciples of all nations' (Mt. 28:19)? How else could the church attest that 'all authority in heaven and in earth' (Mt. 26:18) truly belonged to Jesus? The Old Testament prophecies had clearly pointed to this end-time demonstration of the widest possible horizons of God's mission, yet human restrictions were imposed. We face a continual temptation to appropriate God's revelation to ourselves. Like the Jews, we too would wish to make the eschatological fulfilment all our own. The church's struggle to submit its own self-centred desires to Jesus' commission to share it with the whole world is graphically unfolded in the book of Acts.

The book of Acts begins with Jesus' reaffirmation of his intention that the church's ministry should extend to the ends of the earth. The Holy Spirit comes down to put his seal on the universality of God's redemptive purposes. Today we have understood the gift of tongues in an individualistic sense, ignoring the fact that the pentecostal experience clearly took place within the context of this universalizing of God's mission. The emphasis is not so much on the fact that the disciples began to *speak* in other tongues, as on the fact that God enabled each of the hearers to *hear* the message in his own native language. God in his sovereign control uses all means in order to make his redemptive message heard by all those whom he has intended to hear it. Certainly there are some who are ever hearing but never understanding, and ever seeing but never perceiving, as Isaiah had prophesied (Is. 6:9), but that does not hinder God in continuing to speak to them.

Because Peter was one of those who had a problem with the widening of God's concerns, God gave him an individual vision. Peter's obedience to this vision is depicted as a turning-point in the movement of mission beyond the limits imposed on it by Israel. In obedience to the command of God Peter goes to Cornelius, a Gentile centurion. On meeting a large gathering of relatives and close friends Peter states: 'You are well aware that it is against our law for a Jew to associate with a Gentile or visit him. But God has shown me that I should not call any man impure or unclean' (Acts 10:28).

Two facts need to be underlined. First, in the fulfilling of his kingdom mission, God is in no way restricted. He even bypassed the apostles in sending an angel to deal directly with Cornelius. Secondly, this does not mean, however, that Cornelius could now act on his own, for he needed to relate to the church that God had already started building through his apostles. Having sent for Peter, Cornelius declared, 'We are all here in the presence of God to listen to everything the Lord has commanded you to tell us' (Acts 10:33). God can certainly use all means to declare his message, whether it be in the God–church–world direction or the God–world–church direction. He can certainly bypass the church to act in the world today. If God is truly sovereign he has the liberty to choose how he communicates his concerns. His covenant assures us, however, that he will not ignore the church, which he has appointed as the vehicle by which he will continue to achieve his purposes. In all that is happening, God is preparing his 'bride' for the culminating event when all things will be new (Rev. 21:1–5).

Following this graphic illustration of God's concern, even Peter's Jewish background does not prevent him from accepting God's widening purposes. He responds to Cornelius' testimony with an even clearer testimony: 'I now realise how true it is that God does not show favouritism but accepts men from every nation' (Acts 10:34). Peter goes on to clarify the continuity of the message from its Jewish origins to all who now believe in Jesus, for 'everyone who believes in him receives forgiveness of sins through his name' (10:43).

Luke records that Peter's circumcised companions still had difficulties in accepting this fact. They were 'astonished that the gift of the Holy Spirit had been poured out even on the Gentiles' (10:45). These sceptics probably took back the news to Jerusalem, resulting in Peter's being confronted by the criticism, 'You went into the house of uncircumcised men and ate with them' (11:2). The struggle is obvious, and this despite the fact that God openly poured out his Spirit for them to behold.

Even Peter did not want to take for granted that all would accept what he had been challenged to accept. He took time and carefully 'explained everything to them precisely as it had happened' (11:4). He concludes with a powerful testimony: 'If God gave them the same gift as he gave us, who believed in the Lord Jesus Christ, who was I to think that I could oppose God?' (11:17). A dramatic turn occurred in the minds of the critics as they were led to conclude that 'God has even granted the Gentiles repentance unto life' (11:18).

There are some prejudices that even today the church

has to shed. Sadly, caste and racial barriers still divide the church into high and low, black and white, and even rich and poor. We can hardly blame the early church (which struggled out of deep-rooted traditions and convictions) for the whims and fancies that appear to condition some of our responses today. The prejudice we most urgently need to get rid of is the restriction of the involvement of the people of God within the realms of the church itself.

Without undermining the centrality of God's choice of his church, we need to challenge ourselves to move beyond our limited perspective of the church. With our institutional framework, our denominational distinctives and our limited sacramental views, we have not yet recognized what God is continuing to do through his people outside the four walls of our conceptualization of the church. It is time we expanded our views of the church to see it not only as a worshipping body, but also as a witnessing movement. This understanding will help to break down our restrictions.

It is in Luke's portrayal of Paul that the movement from Jewish to Gentile fields for mission really begins to surface. In fact the entire second half of the book of Acts is basically concerned with this aspect. In the words of F. F. Bruce,

> Rome is the goal towards which the whole of Ac. tends. The Gospel spread out from Palestine in every direction, but the direction in which Luke is interested is the road that leads to Rome. Hence he emphasizes the rise of Gentile evangelization.[3]

Paul had to wait for the church at Antioch to commission him despite the fact that God called him directly to carry the name of the Lord before the Gentiles (Acts 9:15; 13:1–5). Here is yet another emphasis on the role of the church in mission – one that we can so easily neglect. But the even more significant point to note is that the church had matured to the point where it recognized that God's mission knows no bounds of caste, colour, race or sex.

God's purposes had to be accomplished, and the Jews were only the vehicle that, in his sovereign will, he had chosen to use at a particular time in order to fulfil his ultimate purpose.

The 'Jerusalem to Rome' picture of the movement of mission from the Jews to the Gentiles is graphically depicted in Acts as Paul heads towards fulfilling his God-given desire.

> As Rome draws near, the interest thickens, and the climax is reached when Paul is established at the heart of the empire, proclaiming the kingdom of God and teaching the story of the Lord Jesus Christ with all boldness, without let or hindrance – the triumphant peroration *akolytos* expressing Luke's exultation over the situation with which he concludes his work. Here is the final apologetic: not only do the provincial governors place no obstacle in the way of the gospel, but in Rome itself the chief exponent of the gospel is allowed to proclaim it unhindered.[4]

Paul, however, in no way rid himself of a burden for the Jews. He had an intense longing that they would be saved, as can be seen in his letter to the Romans. But the fact that this longing is so intense makes his burden for the Gentiles even more emphatic. 'There is no difference between Jew and Gentile – the same Lord is Lord of all and richly blesses all who call on him' (Rom. 10:12). This conviction brings an even greater significance to the movement from the Jews to the Gentiles.

The movement is clear, and we need to capture its relevance to our discussion. Throughout the history of his dealings with his people, God had challenged them to move forward so that they could come closer to his vision for his world. The struggles of the church in the book of Acts are only symbolic of the deeper struggles that the church faces even today. The barriers we erect are only human and must be constantly and critically evaluated. In so doing, however, we should consider some biblical criteria.

First and foremost, the mission of God calls men and women into a relationship with Jesus Christ so that the world may be reconciled to God. Secondly, God has raised up his church, a community of men and women bound together in their relationship to this one Lord, and it is through this church that he will continue to unfold his mission. In other words, in calling the church to move beyond its boundaries and thereby to be involved in the fullest concern that God has for the world, he is not undermining the people he has already called to be the focal point in the fulfilling of this mission. We are not to be preoccupied with the *channel* he uses for his purposes, but to look beyond it to the *purpose* for which this channel has been created.

The second movement: the reconciliation of all things

The first movement having been accomplished, the New Testament builds up to the second, one which Paul emphasizes – a movement from God's mission to the world to a mission that will show God to be sovereign over all his creation. This is Paul's concern as he writes to the Ephesians and the Colossians about what he refers to as God's 'will . . . to be put into effect when the times will have reached their fulfilment' (Eph. 1:10). Even the movement to the Gentiles seems far too small, for God's mission is now conceived of as concerned with the whole universe.

The fact underlined here is that sin has universal ramifications. In portraying even the universe as being in need of reconciliation, Paul is asserting that the whole universe has been separated from God because of its sin. Peace must be made, oneness must be restored, and this only on the grounds of the shed blood of the Lord Jesus Christ (see Col. 1:20). For Christ's work to be total, its redemptive effects must reach to all of God's created order.

There is, however, no hint of the kind of universalism that implies that all will be absorbed into Christ. On the contrary, Paul asserts the sovereign lordship of Jesus Christ, to whom all things will submit. The entire universe depends on this Saviour, and no other, for its salvation. The complete submission of all creation will bring about the redemption it awaits.

The gospel of the kingdom has been bearing fruit and growing all over the world (Col. 1:6). Even more, it has been proclaimed to every creature under heaven (Col. 1:23), and Paul has been commissioned to accomplish this task. Paul is undoubtedly satisfied that he has been faithful to this commission assigned to him by the risen Lord, but is conscious of an even greater task that God himself is accomplishing through his dominion over all the universe. 'The Christ who is the head of the church is also the fulness of God and Lord of the universe. Church and universe have been joined in the body of Christ.'[5]

Paul points out that God has 'made known to us the mystery of his will according to his good pleasure, which he purposed in Christ, to be put into effect when the times will have reached their fulfilment – to bring all things in heaven and on earth together under one head, even Christ' (Eph. 1:9–10). The horizon of the past that confronts us is that God created all things with the primary intention of demonstrating his lordship, but that human beings conflict with this desire, arrogating lordship to themselves. Creation at present awaits the fulfilment of its Lord's orginally intended purpose. Here again, the totality of God's concern must be taken into account if we are to understand God's desire to restore his creation in his kingdom purposes.

In affirming this emphasis on the lordship of Christ over all things, we must recognize our own small idea of God's mission. God's mission is certainly much bigger than the church's mission, and hence the church's vision must go beyond shortsighted perceptions of a redemption restricted to its own members. We cannot even rest satisfied that the world is now being saved. 'The union of Jew and Gentile in the church becomes a sign and even instrument of the cosmic triumph and reconciliation being effected by God through Jesus Christ.'[6] This is the movement one needs to grasp in order to see the ultimate dimension of God's mission.

The question, however, arises: 'How does the church get involved in this cosmic mission?' In answering it, we must remember, first, that not all of God's mission can be accomplished by the church. His lordship over the entire universe, and in fact in the world, does not imply the church's lordship. It is perhaps a misunderstanding of this lordship that leads us into triumphalistic representations of mission. Yet we need the reminder that the church must be faithful to its role of being all that God wants it to be without limiting itself to narrow perspectives. Committing itself to the lordship of Jesus Christ, it must express itself in servanthood to the world.

We need not fear that in broadening the church's vision we are in any way undermining individual salvation. We should, however, be anxious about restricted views of this salvation. If we can capture even a glimpse of the cosmic backcloth against which individual salvation must be seen, we shall develop a greater appreciation of God's concern for humanity. We must constantly stress the centrality of the community called out by Jesus Christ, consisting of individuals saved by his redemptive work, and in so doing stress how urgent it is for this community to grasp God's cosmic and total concern.

Jesus Christ and creation

Let us consider some aspects of mission that can be drawn from Paul's christology in his letter to the Colossians.

First, Christ is given the central role in all creation, as the one in whom the fulness of the Godhead dwells (Col. 1:19). 'Jesus, as the ultimate personification of God's creative presence, becomes not only the pattern but the very goal towards which creation tends.'[7] Paul highlights the subordination of everything to Christ 'so that in everything he might have the supremacy' (1:18). One of the prime objectives in this assertion is the negation of false beliefs in the created order itself. In Asia and Africa one is well aware of the worship of nature and the fear people live under because of the natural calamities that have caused such devastation. Even the Hellenists thought of nature as a living and divine body, though with God as its ruler.

> Man in this Hellenistic area was not so much worried with his personal problems, his sin and his righteousness, as with the problems of this world, the meaninglessness of life, the threat of an unavoidable fate, the tyranny of heavenly rulers, that is the star that determines every move of earthly life.[8]

Our situation is no different, with similar fears. The message of God's salvation for Asia and Africa needs to stress God's utter supremacy and the absolute subjection of the universe to its Lord.

Paul's emphasis on Jesus Christ's lordship also attacks the dualistic, gnostic assumption that the material is evil and the spiritual good. The Hindu devaluation of creation as *maya*, illusion, is a familiar teaching. Despite recent attempts to redefine it, the concept of an impersonal absolute and a worthless and illusionary creation remains strong.[9] Monistic Hinduism complicates God's role even more by totally identifying God with creation. The biblical God, by contrast, is involved in his creation but stands apart as its Lord. Because men and women in their ignorance and superstition are locked into dualistic or monistic perversions, the mission of the church needs to spell out clearly God's absolute lordship over creation. His lordship assumes that there is nothing inherently evil about creation. His longing for creation's reconciliation, however, and creation's 'groaning' for redemption, confirm that though sin has tainted creation, it can be dealt with on the grounds that God is reconciling the world to himself in Christ (2 Cor. 5:19).

The bold stress on the total humanity of Jesus Christ is another factor we need to consider in dealing with the relationship of God to his creation. God did not see creation as inherently evil, or his Son would not have been allowed to enter creation. He allowed his Son to be manifested as the 'firstborn over all creation' (Col. 1:15) – a title of honour. If God himself so esteems creation, it is surprising that we have not adopted a more positive attitude to it. We have, rather, glibly dismissed ecological concerns as 'liberal' or unrelated to the church. We must, however, always maintain our priorities. When mankind gets right with God it will consequently get right with its world.

Ecological problems have grown large enough to threaten humanity itself. No longer is environmental concern merely an academic exercise, but something that even the world's superpowers are not ignoring. The pressing problems of the greenhouse effect, the depletion of the ozone layer and the loss of plant and animal species all over the world must be tackled at the highest level. The Earth's environmental security is now threatened, and the threat to continued existence itself becomes a major concern. The church is not to become totally preoccupied, however, with the ecological task. Rather, its teaching about God's mission must include an awareness of God's total concern that will encourage its members to get involved in environmental matters at various levels.

Whatever our attitude to ecology, there can hardly be any doubt that at the root of all our problems today lie human greed and selfishness. Hence, even if we hesitate to address ecological crises directly, preaching against human sin itself needs to result in an awakening of conscience that will make us recognize the wide effects of our sinful condition. Reconciliation must begin with the vertical dimension, with people made right with God. That will subsequently bring about a right relationship with our environment.

Jesus Christ and the church

A second aspect of Christ's cosmic lordship is his lordship over the church. In emphasizing his cosmic lordship, we could easily get carried away with the idea of some mythical, all-pervading force as in Greek or Hindu mythologies. The reality of Christ's lordship over all is stressed in order to underline the reality of his lordship over the church. 'The tenor of Christ's lordship is manifested historically and concretely in the community bound to him in love, the church.'[10] In stating that Christ is the head of the body, Paul is asserting that 'the church is the organism through which Christ acts, and which shares all the experiences of Christ.'[11]

The impact of this assertion needs to be spelled out in terms of the church's mission in the world. If Christ is acting through the church today, what is it that the church should be manifesting? Is it truly demonstrating the heart of Christ for lost mankind? Is it demonstrating a concern for the present devastation of creation? Would Christ allow the injustices that have penetrated the very fabric of our world and that consequently influence even the church? We need a total commitment in absolute obedience to allow Christ truly to work through the church today. Mission will be at its best when the church's obedience to its Lord is at its highest.

Positively, we need to note that God places a high premium on the church as his agent to fulfil his mission in the world today. The church, having blunted its edge of true mission, has itself to blame for the rise of the mission agencies or parachurch movements. It is now time for a healthy reversal of this trend. Granting that there is no stopping the mushrooming of mission bodies, the church must accept a corrective. Rather than being critical of such agencies, it must look to the Bible for a fresh understanding of the church itself. The church has been preoccupied with its denominational survival, with its doctrinal separation, and perhaps in some cases even with its effectiveness as a worship centre. But a church that stops at that falls far short of what its Lord desires it to be. It is time, then, for the church to accept the mission agencies as part of God's plan to fulfil his deepest longings for mission to the world. In doing so, the church will not merely seek to duplicate what is already being done, but, acting in healthy cooperation, will offer the soundest corrective for an effective proclamation and demonstration of the gospel.

Jesus Christ and universal reconciliation

Evangelicals have stressed human reconciliation to God, sometimes almost ignoring the wider implications of reconciliation to which the Bible points. The reconciliation depicted in Paul's letters embraces the whole universe. 'The vision of Paul is for a redeemed universe, a universe in which not only the people, but the very things, were redeemed.'[12] Does this mean that God will eventually save all his creation? That is a difficult question.

If God is Lord of all, his mission, too, must be a mission to all. But we must be careful to avoid any confusion between the universalism of certain theologies and the universality that is implied here. Origen's universalism taught that in the end even the devil and all his angels would be reconciled. While God's mission is to all, not everyone may be willing to subject himself or herself to his control. The New Testament makes it amply clear that an intelligent commitment is involved between the one reconciled and the reconciler. Hence God's kingdom concern does not automatically assume that all will be reconciled. All we can say is that his primary purposes are directed towards mankind, and that all those who commit themselves to him will be redeemed.

However these things may be, this much is certain: God's only aim was to reconcile men to himself in Jesus Christ; the medium by which he did so was the death of Christ which proved that there were no limits to his love, and that reconciliation extends to all the universe, in earth and heaven alike.[13]

The church and God's cosmic mission

The cosmic scope of God's mission is set in its proper perspective in Paul's splendid introduction to his letter to the Ephesians (1:1–23). The universal dimension of the kingdom mission is spelled out, and the responsibility and privilege of the church are underlined – the church not only possesses the ultimate plan of God, but also proclaims it. The church has been blessed with insight into God's plan for his whole universe.

Here again, Paul does not allow the cosmic scope of Jesus Christ to remain at some abstract, philosophical level, but shows it to be real by pointing to the gracious inclusion of the Gentiles, who are 'no longer foreigners and aliens but fellow-citizens with God's people' (Eph. 2:19). This bringing together of Jew and Gentile is an observable demonstration of the bringing together of 'all things in heaven and on earth . . . under one head, even Christ' (1:10). This reconciliation is made concrete in the church, powerfully implying that in God's plan and purpose, missiology and ecclesiology go hand in hand. The church is not the end of God's mission; it is only the means by which he will fulfil the universal reconciliation.

The fact that is repeatedly underlined is that the church must be involved in the fullest possible expression of God's kingdom mission if it is truly to be the church. It can claim no exemption on any grounds. Paul's ecclesiology reminds the church of its prime purpose – to be involved in God's ultimate plans through his redemptive mission, and in so doing to find its place in Christ, in whom 'the whole building is joined together and rises to become a holy temple in the Lord' (Eph. 2:21).

Not even this reference to the building up of the church sanctions the appropriation of these gifts for its own benefit. Rather, they are given so that God's ultimate intention may be fulfilled – that 'through the church, the manifold wisdom of God should be made known' (3:10). The church in worship is not an end in itself; the building up is for a more powerful witness. We should, however, avoid an over-emphasis on either side that could only result in an incomplete and ineffective church. For instance, there are churches that get so caught up in mission that they place inadequate stress on worship. This results in a weak witness. In order to be a powerful witness, the church must strengthen itself through its worship.

The key to drawing out the depths of Paul's concern in the letter to the Ephesians is to understand the close link between the cosmic scope of God's kingdom mission and the centrality of the church in making known this total plan. God's reconciling purposes for all, demonstrated in the establishing of his redeemed community, are declared through a people in worship committed to a mission that witnesses to God's ultimate purposes. The church must resist the temptation to neglect the proclamation it is called to make. A mission that does not proclaim God's redemptive purposes for humanity can only result in an incomplete mission.

One other movement could be mentioned in passing. There is a historical continuity to the church in mission. The coming together of the Jews and Gentiles in God's eternal plan is based on the historical 'foundation of the apostles and the prophets, with Christ Jesus himself as the chief cornerstone' (2:20).

There is no need to attempt to re-establish 'New Testament churches' today. I am amazed at the continuing call to go back to the New Testament church. We need to explode the myth of the New Testament church by reminding ourselves that it too had problems just as we do. It was a far from perfect church. Rather, we should note the continuity of history. The church is ever growing in its quest increasingly to become the body that glorifies the Lord. It learns lessons, sometimes through utter failure, but all these are part of a continuous growth. Even the perversions and heresies that arise within this body set before us warnings that are helpful in this process of growth.

Paul's prayer for the church

The powerful prayer of Paul in Ephesians 1:17–19a includes some significant petitions that bear on our present considerations. First, Paul prays for the Spirit of wisdom to be given to the church. Wisdom has a variety of meanings in Scripture – unusual ability and knowledge, specialized knowledge, and judicial shrewdness, among others. In the gospels it is generally 'tied to the traditional OT and Jewish conception, where wisdom is man's approach to life, arising out of his life in the covenant bestowed by God'.[14]

Paul's first letter to the Corinthians contrasts the wisdom of this world with the wisdom of the cross. The cross seemed to be foolishness in the light of human wisdom (1 Cor. 1:18–25) but God in his infinite wisdom cut across human wisdom to reveal to us 'the mystery of his will' (Eph. 1:9). This wisdom is not merely a particular insight, but an access to God's will enabling us to know him and his purposes. It is those who 'have the mind of Christ' (1 Cor. 2:16) that are able to appreciate the deepest significance of this privilege.

Paul's prayer for the Ephesian believers implies that this wisdom is not something acquired through one's own abilities, but is a gracious gift from God himself that will enable us to 'know him better' (Eph. 1:17). This reminder needs to come to us afresh in a day when human speculations are replacing the Spirit-led manifestations of God's mission. The wisdom and knowledge that lead to a better knowledge of God himself are by far the greatest need for anyone involved in understanding and acting on God's redemptive concern for the world today. In our stress on contextualizing the message, we have placed little emphasis on the fact that the message should first impact the life of the messenger himself or herself. The need to actualize our theology, to work it out in practice, will lead to a far more effective involvement in mission.

Some current theologies so confront us with human rationalization that God appears to be on the periphery of the exercise. Even so-called evangelical attempts to promote mission cause concern when they are devised in keeping with the modern preoccupation with success, with strategies evolved to maximize the end result, rather than out of a longing to be faithful to God's desires for each situation. The financial and technological resources available to modern missiologists can easily degrade mission to become an exercise in manipulating immediate results as an alternative to awaiting the fulfilment of God's ultimate purposes in his time.

In its structured formulations and traditional, repeatable models, worked out with little sensitivity to God's desires for each particular context, mission can stifle the newness of God's work in each situation. The early church realized the importance of waiting for God to empower them before they embarked on their mission. They had no neatly worked out plans, and could not draw upon the enormous resources available today. Yet the results were phenomenal. We should not take this to mean that the most successful missions are the least structured! We could err even more on that side. The church today needs to appropriate the wisdom of God in a fuller way in order to comprehend how God's plans can be made real afresh in its life and mission today.

8

The missiology of John

We have emphasized the fact that God's mission is his message actualized in a real world – a world of people within a God-created environment. The idea of this world is much more clearly developed in John's gospel than in the synoptics, and so we shall explore some Johannine themes that relate to a theology of mission. These themes are interlinked. For instance, once we understand John's cosmology we are in a much better position to understand his christology and soteriology. It is surprising that, despite John's extensive and varied handling of the concept of the world (*kosmos*), some dismiss his gospel as having little missiological value.

John has a clearly defined evangelistic objective in writing. 'These are written that you may believe that Jesus is the Christ, the Son of God, and that by believing you may have life in his name' (20:31). He wants his readers to believe that Jesus is the Messiah, for in doing so they will have life. Some have suggested that John is thus not concerned so much with historical facts as with theology. This may be so, but we have already stressed that there need be no conflict between theology and history. John certainly interprets facts, but to assume that history is not to be interpreted is to revert to nineteenth-century positivistic attitudes which attempted to see history as bloodless facts. There is adequate scholarship to sustain the belief that John shows no disrespect for history. His references to times, places and events bear witness to this. Our problem arises because we are obliged to read first-century writings with twentieth-century eyes, and this is inevitably frustrating. Even if we read the gospel from a present-day perspective, we must first and foremost understand the writer's objective at the time.

Basically, we need to accept that John is interested in something far more than history. Both John's christology and his soteriology are cosmic in scope. If he pays less attention to factual detail than, say, Mark does, it is because John's purposes are cosmological in their dimension. While the other gospels speak in terms of the kingdom, John utilizes the symbol of the cosmos and Jesus' relevance to all humanity. Yet in so doing, John anchors the cosmic mission soundly in historical fact. Jesus Christ is thus 'the Saviour of the world' (4:42), 'the light of the world' (8:12; 9:5), and the 'bread' given 'for the life of the world' (6:51).

The second aspect of John's assertion is the fact of the universality of God's salvation. It is not to be restricted to the Jews or to those who can gain access into Jewish circles. Thus, John is later able to develop the thought that 'God so loved the world' and that 'whoever believes' will qualify for the life that God gives (3:16). God's concern is not for a chosen few but for all that he has created. The universal and cosmological stress is present right from the start of John's gospel.

The universality of salvation refutes our present-day ideas of universalism. In our preoccupation with inclusivistic ideas of dialogue we have tended to accept that, with the historic cultural changes of today, it would be unacceptable to ascribe superiority to the Christian revelation. The question we must ask, however, is not whether it is acceptable to modern people, but whether it is consonant with the biblical claim. That is the kind of biblical theology we are attempting to draw out for mission.

Contrary to the belief that John is not interested in history, we are reminded that Jesus is a historical figure, attested by the historical John the Baptist. It is through this one who came into the world that life, true light, authentic fellowship with God and the fulfilment of ultimate cosmic purposes are made possible. There is no doubt that John is more preoccupied with theology than with a mere retelling of facts, but this in no way diminishes his concern for a real historical gospel. Affirming Jesus' historical reality, he goes on to demonstrate far greater dimensions of Jesus' influence. Hence cosmic concerns become the focus of John's attention.

Jesus Christ as the Word of God

John's introduction, with its reference to the *logos,* or *Word*, underlines this cosmic interest. This all-pervading, rational principle of the world has now been made flesh and blood to bring rationality to mankind. Whatever we judge to be the meaning of *logos*, the term was clearly significant to John's readers. But John's intention is to show that what was thought to be detached from and unconcerned about this world has now entered the arena of history to give practical outworking to God's redemptive purposes for humanity.

This practical outworking of God's concern is itself the most adequate model for mission. So much missionary action lacks an adequate biblical foundation. Mission is God's Word made real to the world. This is the central message of John's prologue. The God who created the world is the one who cares for the world now in darkness. This concern is expressed not in words only, but also in becoming flesh in order to demonstrate the grace and truth of God.

Some have attempted to draw parallels between the *logos* and the Hindu *Om*. In the *Upanishads*, *Om* is said to be all that was, all that is and all that will be. It is the unique sound in which God utters all that he utters. It may be permissible to draw such parallels as long as we do not infer that the two terms refer to one and the same thing. In fact, there is hardly any comparison, for John utilizes the term to depict God's incarnation and identification with the struggles of this world, and this allows no room for comparison with the 'all-pervading force' which continues to abide in eternity.

John's emphasis on God's mission relates to a God who

is interested in real human beings in actual history and seeks to identify with them personally. We have already attempted to stress the personal nature of the biblical God, and this needs to be asserted again. Only a personal God can reveal himself personally and also identify with the joys and struggles of mankind. One of the most potent arguments against the god of New Age religion is the personal nature of the biblical God.

Moreover, it is clear that in speaking about the Word, John is not referring to something distinct from God, or even to the words or activity of God. It is God himself expressing himself totally in Jesus Christ. 'The Word was God' (Jn. 1:1). John ascribes personality to the Word, in contrast to the static utterances of whatever parallels we wish to draw. This is not just an affirmation of divinity but also a confirmation of identity. A theology of mission must take this fact into account to point to the total involvement of God who desires to express all of himself concretely in his message to the world.

The *logos* and creation

In developing our thesis on mission from the kingdom perspective, we have implicitly stressed the foundational element of the creator God who manifests himself as the redeemer God. This element is nowhere more clearly stressed in the New Testament than in John's prologue. And the *logos* theme proceeds naturally into the creation theme: 'Through him all things were made; without him nothing was made that has been made' (1:3). The fact that everything owes its existence to God is the premise on which God builds his concern for all things. 'The whole creation is included in one broad sweep. Nothing is outside the range of his activity.'[1] Here we have a powerful antidote to any illusory (*maya*) understanding of creation and ultimately the implication of unreality. The world is reality as God meant it to be, and hence it is worthy of God's personal involvement.

We may be justified in repeating our emphasis on a more

positive attitude to creation. The Hindu and Buddhist attitudes, like those of the ancient Near East, basically identify impermanence with meaninglessness. There is no doubt that creation is subject to decay and hence is impermanent. The biblical fact of a God who deliberately created, however, includes the idea that he thereby invests meaningfulness into created things. There is purpose in his involvement with mankind and the created order.

This stress is lacking in Hindu teaching. 'Brahman is impersonal . . . the world is not only worthless as compared to Brahman but in its very truth illusion, maya.'[2] Both personality and creativity are devalued. John in his time was dealing with ideas of early gnosticism which attributed such negative properties to creation. 'The world is due to God himself acting through his word.'[3] If this is true, God takes full responsibility for creation, and so his redeemed children should act responsibly towards God's created world.

Ecological concerns are not to be shunned by well-meaning evangelicals who may fear that such concern will dilute their understanding of God's redemptive intentions for humanity. Even if we do not regard a concern for creation as a legitimate aspect of God's mission, we should at least accept that it ought to be a Christian concern. If Bible-believing Christians avoid ecological involvement, non-Christians will take it over. John points us to a positive attitude towards God's creation.

Life and light

The object of God's mission in relation to our world today has to be tangibly experienced. This is John's concern as he develops his account of Jesus' mission to impart life. The *logos* life has been made real and visible in a human life. Even a casual reading of the gospel will call to attention the stress on the concept of life which is peculiar to John. Life is not an accident, or even something that exists of itself. There is an intrinsic connection between Jesus and life, and this is outlined frequently. This life is 'the light of men' (1:4); it is 'eternal life' (3:16) and 'life to the full' (10:10). Only those who come to Jesus really have life (5:40).

The question of the meaning of life is universally asked. Where have I come from? Where am I going? What is the significance of life now? Missiology must handle such questions and be able to make men and women understand such basic issues. Perhaps the fact that Transcendental Meditation purports to answer such questions contributes to its success. Hinduism itself will not accept that all are capable of true life. Only the privileged upper caste can have any claim to life in its fulness. In contrast, the Maharishi Mahesh Yogi entices people by saying that human beings are born to live a perfect life, encompassing the values of the transcendental absolute. According to the Maharishi, the two ways of life, the relative and the absolute, need to be brought together, and this union will produce 200% life. Abundant life is the fundamental issue in John's writings; he wrote his gospel so that by believing in Jesus people might have life in Jesus' name (20:31). This is life in all its fulness.

Perhaps the most forceful attack upon the evolutionary hypothesis is that it ignores the uniqueness of humanity and the quality of human life. The biblical teaching that humanity is distinct from and superior to the rest of the created world must be taken into account. The distinctiveness is qualitative, and has to do with the essence of life that humanity has access to, being made in the image of God. This life has been affected by the fall, and consequently the mission of Jesus is to restore this qualitative aspect of human existence. 'I have come that they may have life, and have it to the full' (Jn. 10:10).

The mission of God in sending Jesus to restore true life is explicitly stated in John and must be fully explored in our evangelistic message. We constantly speak of the need to make the gospel relevant to the local context, and perhaps in doing so we have focused on socio-economic issues. The question of life, being so fundamental to human existence, provides us with a point of relevance to all. It is into this broad context that the gospel has to be expressed.

Pessimism is characteristic of people today. With so much suffering, conflict and tension in the world, this is hardly surprising. Gloom and despair drive people either to believe that there is nothing beyond what is observable, or to feel that beyond all this seeming meaninglessness there must be some purpose. It is not surprising that people want to dismiss this world as an illusion.

Marxist philosophy is really an attempt to look beyond for meaning. The individual trapped within the capitalist environment can find fulfilment when he ultimately frees himself into the new society. Human problems are brought about by an oppressive and evil society that exploits people. The Christian recognizes the evil structures of this world as being part of the reason for his struggles with the meaning of life. But he goes even further by recognizing that humanity itself is part of that problem.

The eternal life that Jesus gives is not just a future hope, but a quality of life in relation to God in the present. John tells us that this eternal life is ours when we 'remain in the Son and in the Father' (1 Jn. 2:24). God's mission is not to clean up our environment and in so doing clean us up too. His ultimate desire is to bring us back into a purposeful relationship with himself. 'Remain in me, and I will remain in you,' Jesus reminded his disciples (Jn. 15:4).

Not everyone is capable of philosophizing and rationalizing about ultimate questions. To many in this world, life is merely the opposite of death. The Bible is not oblivious of this fact and constantly seeks to address the issue. Desperate people are willing to pay any price to prolong life, but despite all the advances in modern medicine we are utterly frustrated by the inevitability of death. It is true that we have increased our life expectancy. But the question is whether our *quality* of life has been improved. In many cases all that medicine achieves is the prolongation of death.

We are the only creatures who know we must die. This prompts us to wonder whether there is life beyond death. John addresses this preoccupation. 'Whoever believes in him shall not perish but have eternal life' (Jn. 3:16). Eternal life refers to the quality rather than to the quantity of life, though Jesus also promises everlasting life.

The question of death leads to the question of the wholeness of the individual. Dominated by the Greek concept of the immortality of the soul, popular Christian belief has regarded eternal life as the continuation of soul-life after bodily death. Even the more theologically sophisticated have often tended to use dualistic language about 'body' and 'soul'. We have even stressed the need to be more concerned for the soul than for the body. I do not want to take this further here. Suffice it to say that this attitude contributes to the limiting of evangelism to something concerned only with the soul, and to the avoidance of involvement in God's material world.

Human beings are neither bodiless souls nor soulless bodies. The biblical teaching, particularly in the Old Testament, is clear that we are one whole. So life after death must in some way be a continuation of the life of the whole person. This cuts right across the Hindu belief in the independent existence of the soul and its ability to be transferred into any number of bodies. The human being is one whole, so the promise of eternal life must also assure him of wholeness.

John is not concerned with mere soul-talk. He is concerned with a Jesus who relates to real people, offering them living water (Jn. 4:10), the bread of life (6:35), and the way, the truth and the life (14:6). Jesus is talking not about the soul or existence but about life in contrast to death. Since he has 'life in himself' (5:26), he can remedy the lack of life in us. Knowing Jesus is directly related to knowing life.

Since the issue of life is central to people in every situation, mission must stress the centrality of God's concern to touch life in all its aspects. Any lessening of this will be unbiblical. It is for this reason that God sent Jesus into the world, and consequently it is for this reason that Jesus sends his disciples into this same world. The reality of the biblical message is tested by its relevance to every aspect of life.

The concept of the world

The mission or 'sent-ness' of Jesus Christ is a clear feature of John's gospel. Just as Jesus was sent, so also his disciples are sent to accomplish God's mission. 'As the Father has sent me, I am sending you' (20:21). This is the Johannine equivalent of the Great Commission in Matthew 28:18–20. Jesus sent his disciples into the world to fulfil the task God entrusted to him. Jesus came into the world (1:10–11) in response to God's love for the world (3:16), and his disciples are to go into the world in the same way.

A variety of meanings

The concept of 'the world' embraces a variety of meanings in John's gospel.

First, it refers to the ordered universe. 'The world was made through him' (1:10). The basic meaning of the word *kosmos* is 'an ornament', something beautifully built and artistically arranged. This meaning is at the root of the English word 'cosmetic'. 'The universe with all its harmonious relationships is the outstanding ornament.'[4] Jesus uses the word in this sense when he prays: 'Glorify me in your presence with the glory I had with you before the world began' (17:5). It is a glorious fact that the entire universe in all its orderliness was created through Christ. But 'for men, this earth is the most significant part of the universe, so it is not surprising that the term came to be used for this world in which we live'.[5] It is interesting to note that the Greeks used *kosmos* to refer also to the heavens.

A second meaning of 'world' in Johannine usage refers to its human inhabitants. This 'world' is the object of God's love (3:16). He loved mankind, his creation, so much that he sent his Son to live among them. This clearly emphasizes the centrality of men and women in God's created order. God's redemption is directed primarily towards human beings, and his salvific blessings are primarily for 'whoever believes in him' (3:16). It is through the salvation of men and women that the rest of creation will receive God's redemptive benefits. Mission that focuses in an abstract way on social structures and ecological concerns cannot be justified biblically. John's emphasis is on the concreteness of God's mission to a world of people who need to be redeemed.

The biblical term 'world', then, is not totally negative. We often use the word 'worldliness' to mean what is contrary to Christ's desires. This needs to be corrected. The word has a positive meaning that we need to underline in our thinking about God's mission to the world. We often misinterpret biblical spirituality as alienation from this world. This leads to an attitude of superiority and condescension in effecting our mission. There is a kind of 'worldliness' that we need to restore, whereby the church in mission would recognize that it belongs to the world and would thereby demonstrate the incarnational mission of God to humanity.

The world as the object of God's mission, and hence Christ's incarnation, must remind us that we Christians belong to humankind and that we and the rest of humanity are created in the image of God. God is concerned with all who are created in his image. And our mission to the world, if it is to be in keeping with God's mission to the world, must be firmly established on this foundation. Many non-Christians complain that we approach them with a superior attitude, sometimes, sadly, referred to as the 'missionary mentality'. We must dispel this attitude by appreciating that the Bible speaks of communication by identification. John emphasizes that Jesus 'came to that which was his own' (1:11).

Mission conducted in this way will more effectively communicate the redemptive intentions of God. While the modern missionary movement is to be acclaimed for the sacrificial part it has played in bringing salvation to millions all over the world, it is true that in many cases total identification was lacking. This was to some extent inevitable as the 'civilized' westerner took the gospel to 'less developed' peoples. Because it is hard to integrate into an alien culture, we imported some of our own culture into local cultures, often adopting a condemnatory attitude towards them. This should remind us to cultivate a greater sensitivity to people, their culture and tradition. There are no superior and inferior cultures as far as God is concerned. He cuts across all cultures in order to incarnate his message.

Opposition to God

Having emphasized the positive aspects of the 'world', we must not neglect the negative. John emphasizes that the world is the realm of evil, at enmity with God.[6] This new meaning that the term 'world' acquires in the New Testament brings out the sharp contrast between the beauty of God's creation and the ugliness of human sin. As John sees it, the men and women who inhabit this beautiful world have acted in an ugly manner, this ugliness becoming all the more highlighted when brought face to face with Jesus Christ. Human sinfulness cannot confront the perfection of Christ and his righteous demands. People therefore experience discomfort, even hatred for Christ, when he confronts their evil (Jn. 7:7).

Triumphalistic ideas of mission tend to gloss over this very important depiction of the world in relation to Christ. Because the world resists the things of God, set plans for winning converts and planting churches may not always work. One wonders whether the goal-setting and strategy-planning of our mission programmes have been taken a bit too far. This does not mean that we should discard all goals and strategies, but that we must submit our plans to the will of God as well as recognize the resistance of a world under Satan.

This resistance is not just apathy to Christ, but rejection of and even antagonism to his claims. Missionaries in fields where satanic forces are more noticeably at work are familiar with this kind of opposition. It is to be expected as Jesus judges 'the prince of this world' (Jn. 12:31). John makes it very clear that 'the whole world is under the control of the evil one' (1 Jn. 5:19). Since Satan has a hold on this world, it naturally opposes Christ. The phenomenon of demon possession even today is one extreme demonstration of satanic influence, and confrontation with Christ in such situations results in open conflict.

Luke records the amazement of the crowds when Jesus cast out a demon, and the Pharisees' response: 'By Beelzebub, the prince of demons, he is driving out demons' (Lk. 11:14). Jesus counters this with a simple but powerful argument – if the devils themselves can cast one another out then their kingdom will not stand. 'But if I drive out demons by the finger of God, then the kingdom of God has come to you' (11:20).

> This passage is not an isolated one. The whole struggle of Jesus against the devils is determined by the antithesis between the kingdom of heaven and the rule of Satan, and time and time again Jesus' superior power over Satan and Satan's dominion proves the breakthrough on the part of the kingdom of God.[7]

The conflict on the mission field is a kingdom conflict and hence the dominion of the devil will violently react against the authority of Jesus. Those at the cutting edge of mission must expect hatred, opposition, conflict, violence, antagonism and all kinds of demonstrations against the purposes of God as he establishes his kingdom through the redemptive ministry of Jesus Christ and through the Holy Spirit. John emphasizes that the Spirit convicts the world of sin and guilt as 'the prince of this world now stands condemned' (Jn. 16:11).

John also portrays the world as an evil system standing against Christ. When he pleads with the early Christians not to 'love the world or anything in the world' (1 Jn. 2:15), he refers to the principles, the attitudes or the evil system of this world. 'For everything in the world – the cravings of sinful man, the lust of his eyes and the boasting of what he has and does – comes not from the Father but from the world' (1 Jn. 2:16). Jesus uses the word in this sense when he tells the Jewish leaders that they are 'of this world' (Jn. 8:23). Those who have the spirit of 'antichrist' speak 'from the viewpoint of the world' (1 Jn. 4:5).

Our involvement in the world

God's kingdom mission confronts the kingdom of Satan manifest in the evil that has penetrated the very structures of this world. The so-called liberation theologies have advocated the transformation of existing evil structures. Such theologies criticize individualistic ideas of sin which have flourished in capitalist societies to the neglect of structural evils within their systems. The existing structures have only aided the oppressor and increased injustices.

Liberation theologians issue a call to struggle against oppressive structures and to construct a more just society. They also call us to turn away from a preoccupation with sin, regarding it as an impediment to the experience of the afterlife.

> Insofar as it constitutes a break with God, sin is a historical reality, it is a breach of the communion of man with each other, it is a turning in of man on himself which manifests itself in a multifaceted withdrawal from others. And because sin is a personal and social intra-historical reality, a part of the daily events of human life, it is also, and above all, an obstacle to life's reaching the fulness we call salvation.[8]

We should rather, they argue, be concerned with the religious significance of human action in history.

> The grace–sin conflict, the coming of the kingdom, and the expectation of the parousia are all

necessarily and inevitably historical, temporary, earthly, social and material realities.[9]

We are told that because of our traditional ideas of sin, spirituality and worldliness, we have ignored the cry of the prophets against sinful structures. Choan-Seng Song writes:

A poorly understood spiritualization has often made us forget the human consequences of the eschatological promises and the power to transform unjust social structures which they imply. The elimination of misery and exploitation is a sign of the coming of the kingdom.[10]

On the positive side, we appreciate the concern to expose the evil systems of this world, about which John is definitely concerned. If we accept the fallenness of man we must also accept the fallenness of the world. Mission must concern itself with addressing the fallen structures of this world. Our spirituality has been too unreal and other-worldly, and we have seen the world as a fallen realm which we have no spiritual sanction to enter. How soon we forget Jesus' words: 'My prayer is not that you take them out of the world but that you protect them from the evil one' (Jn. 17:15)! Jesus asserted that we 'are not of the world' (17:14), that is, we do not belong to the systems of this world. We have developed this into an individualized spirituality which insulates us from the rest of the world.

Mission must be conducted in the context of God's message of the kingdom to the world. Choan-Seng Song pleads for a 'mission of enfleshment',[11] the kind of mission that accepts that the 'God of creation is the God of incarnation'.[12] This is seen as the basic message of the prologue to the fourth gospel. John grasps the mystery of all mysteries, namely God's mission of enfleshment. 'World history is part of the totality embraced by the framework of creation and incarnation.'[13] Therefore, Christian mission, we are reminded, must reflect the nature and essence of such an enfleshment.

Song recommends that the first step we should take is that of becoming almost everything the church has so far forbidden itself to become. The church's western identity is blamed for this.[14]

> The chief task of Christian mission is to let the faith in Jesus Christ become the element which enables civilizations to be renewed as witness to the glory of God's creation and manifestation of the presence of God as Saviour in the world.[15]

Civilization itself, the world we have abhorred as in opposition to the Christian world, needs to be renewed, not merely Christianized.

Secondly, 'God's mission of enfleshment means that God has now become available to humanity. Jesus Christ is this availability of God.'[16] In Jesus Christ, God stands where we stand. We cannot therefore go to the world armed with our doctrinal orthodoxy, value judgments, cultural immunity or moral standards. 'You must be ready to accept their standards as your standards, their values as your values, their sin as your sin.'[17] Song, writing from a Chinese perspective, betrays an anti-western-missionary attitude, accepting that 'the communist use of power in China was God's judgment upon the flabby church.'[18] Nevertheless, Song is keen to stress that the focus of Christian mission should be Christ in the context of this world.

The confusion arises over where we draw the line between what Christian mission offers to the world and what the world already is in itself, without the Christian mission. Even if it is to receive something through this mission, it seems on this view as though it can arrive at it without Christ. All that our Christian influence appears to do is alleviate the situation in the world rather than bring the world to any commitment to Christ. This vague notion of mission as enfleshment leaves us wondering what the uniqueness of the Christian mission is all about.

The mission of the kingdom adds the future horizon to all our efforts, giving them a quality beyond what we ourselves can achieve. It is a movement towards the ultimate fulfilment of God's purposes in God's time. The future horizon totally controls our present horizon. All that the church should be is conditioned by all that it will ultimately become in God's kingdom. Any missiology written purely out of a desire to correct past faults is in danger of neglecting the kingdom perspective that the Bible emphasizes.

John is clear that Jesus Christ sends his disciples into the world to contribute something unique – the message of the future life already available to the believer in the present. This message is concrete and life-changing. Those who accept this message experience a changed relationship to God, which subsequently changes their relationship to the world. The message is not only about a spiritual, future life, but about eternal life here and now.

In depicting the evil systems of the world, resulting from human sin, however, John does not portray a God who condemns this world. Rather, because of his love, God desires the world to be saved (3:17). John the Baptist, announcing the coming of Jesus Christ, cries: 'Look, the Lamb of God, who takes away the sin of the world!' (1:29). Nicodemus hears of the God who so loves the world that he sends Jesus. Such passages remind us of God's passionate concern to save the world. Mission that cannot present this God will fail to demonstrate the mission of God fully and in concrete ways.

Our identity in the world

According to John, then, the world is very much God's ultimate concern. Having created it in beauty and orderliness, he wants to redeem it. Salvation in this sense is a restoration of beauty and orderliness. Human beings have fallen from the glory of God, and God's mission is to restore this glory. Because of human sinfulness, even the created order has been subjected to decay and disorder. God's redemptive purposes have to do with the restoration of the order that he desires for his whole creation. All that God had intended when he made the world is now to be made real in the mission of his Son. Christians must therefore identify with the world as Christ did in his incarnation. Christians have attempted to stand apart from the world and have thus failed truly to communicate God's loving heart to the world today.

The church must recognize that it belongs to the world. It should not retreat into an unreal spirituality or an otherworldly superiority, but should show itself to be composed of real people in a real world. Too often we have behaved as though we were some kind of alien species, sent here to show 'love' to the world from outside. This kind of attitude has hindered true identification. The over-emphasis on cross-cultural mission tends to perpetuate this impression of Christians identifying with something that is alien to them. This has led to condescension on the part of some missionaries, which has hindered the gospel. It is time for the church to recognize that its mission is 'intra-cultural'. Similarly, calls for indigenization and contextualization refer to purely human attempts to make the message relevant. When God truly speaks, his message is made concrete, and this actualization of the message needs to be spontaneously demonstrated in mission.

A further word needs to be added in relation to mission within culture. If we are to take seriously Jesus' sending us into the world just as he was sent into it, the church must identify itself more concretely with the cultures and nations in which it finds itself. We have almost behaved as though there were a universal Christian culture distinct from 'non-Christian' cultures. Unfortunately, this 'Christian culture' is often synonymous with western culture. We need to understand our own cultures in an effort to communicate Jesus Christ within our own setting. This far more natural process of communication could be referred to as our 'intra-cultural' mission. This in no way stands in opposition to 'cross-cultural' mission, but only rectifies an imbalance. Given the history of missions, one can accept that in many countries the church needs to flesh out its message within its own culture before it can be challenged to cross cultural barriers to communicate the message.

Culture is embraced within God's concern for his people, and, as we have seen in discussing creation, God himself introduced the elements of a good culture. Humanity's fall results in culture's fall, but salvation in Jesus Christ in no way draws people away from their culture. Jesus Christ fully identified with contemporary Jewish culture, not because it was perfect, but because it was his. The fact that he sends us into the world implies that he has called us to be part of our own cultures and thereby to contribute to the eventual redemption of culture as it is brought into line with kingdom culture.

Secondly, we need to contribute in more practical ways to the process of the redemption of God's world. I am not thinking of the ideas underlying nineteenth-century kingdom theologies which spoke of a social gospel that could bring about the kingdom here on earth. In contrast, the Christian, belonging to God's world, ought to be exercising a positive influence within it. The preoccupation with the preaching of the gospel without an equally strong emphasis on the demonstration of this life-changing good news has been severely criticized by non-Christians who have sincerely sought to assess the validity of our claims. It is time for the church to awake out of its complacency and make an impact that demonstrates the message we are called to preach.

Getting involved in changing the structures of this world is a concrete expression of the gospel of Jesus Christ. Such an expression will enable us to hold together the three horizons that we have referred to as the kingdom concern. The anticipation of the fulfilment of God's purposes in his kingdom gives mission a complete perspective that is lacking in purely human causes. It is, then, wrong to attack such social efforts as unbiblical. Wilberforce in England, Pandita Ramabai in India, and many others, confronted not only personal sin but also its influence on the systems of this world. These are not wasted efforts, but display God's concern for the world. In our over-reaction to a one-sided stress on changing evil structures, we have sat back in non-involvement. There is no justification for this kind of resignation. Christ gave himself for the sinful world, and we too must be willing to give ourselves in every way as a demonstration of Christlike concern for the world.

The fallacy lies in seeing mission as nothing but involvement in the world's systems and in maintaining that the church everywhere should be involved in attacking evil structures. At the most, this could be the calling of an individual Christian or perhaps of a particular church in a particular situation. John's message of the new birth implies God's concern to get to the very root of structural evil. John 3:3 employs the phrase 'born again' or 'born from above', which could imply that even structures can be changed as they are renewed through submission to Jesus Christ. This phrase confused Nicodemus. The kingdom of God demands a radical change in anyone seeking to enter it. External cleansing and clearing out of structures is not sufficient. Jesus made very clear to Nicodemus that it is the Spirit who will bring about this newness. The change will come not by human effort but by God's own intervention. Moreover, since humanity's fall resulted in sinful structures, only in humanity's redemption can these structures be transformed.

God's kingdom concern starts with human renewal setting people on course for life in the kingdom. This new status itself brings a new dimension to mission. The new person desires to bring about new structures in keeping with his kingdom concern. Attacking structural sin is abstract, but renewing humankind is the concrete mission that God has called us to participate in. John's gospel emphasizes a tangible world of people to whom God demonstrates his love. We shall certainly experience structural changes in the new heaven and the new earth. But the world as the object of God's love is a world of people, not an abstract system or structure – however acutely those systems and structures need God's intervention. God's kingdom mission, however, penetrates even abstract systems when his concerns are made real to real people in a real world.

9

The role of the Holy Spirit

In our search for biblical themes that will assist in developing a solid missiological foundation for the church's witness today, we inevitably come to the work of the Holy Spirit. In fact, it is hardly possible to deal with the work of the Spirit as a just section of our considerations, given the foundational role that is ascribed to him in the Bible.

Roland Allen, writing more than four decades ago, challenged us to restore to the Holy Spirit his rightful role 'primarily as the dictator and inspirer of missionary work'.[1] So penetrating is his reminder about the ministry of the Holy Spirit that it is regrettable that his words have not been more widely heeded. With all our programmatic approaches to mission we have unconsciously 'turned the divine initiative into a human enterprise', as John Taylor puts it.[2]

Mission today betrays an overwhelmingly action-oriented approach to the fulfilling of God's purposes. Triumphalistic agendas and success-centred formulations smack of the manipulative tendencies of the business world rather than of the miraculous work of the Holy Spirit evidenced in the book of Acts. When we give the Spirit his proper place in the missionary movement we will put the role of God's people in its rightful place alongside the divine initiative which impels mission. There is certainly a human element in mission, but it must be seen from the perspective of the Holy Spirit's function in the divine programme.

For instance, Roland Allen, referring to the description of the book of Acts as the 'Acts of the Holy Spirit' points out that this description is one-sided in that it 'obscures the human element'.[3]

The apostles were men. Their acts were their own acts. They were not mere will-less instruments in the hands of another. Nevertheless, the fact that it was possible to call the Acts of the Apostles the 'Acts of the Holy Spirit' reveals at once the truth that men have found in this book not merely the record of the acts of men, but the revelation of a Spirit governing, guiding, controlling, directing men in the acts here recorded.[4]

Allen is careful to point out that Luke writes about people liable to human errors and passions, who nevertheless were 'recipients of a gift of the Holy Spirit'.[5] This reminder about the role of the Spirit must be emphasized as a corrective to any wrong emphases that we may discern in mission today. The world we live in, with its revolution in information technology, could easily favour static approaches to mission. Moreover, in keeping with the action-oriented generation, the programme prescribed for the church today is primarily one of continuing motion.

We may be rather shocked to discover that the Great Commission of Matthew 28:19, 'Go . . . and make disciples,' has not always been the motivation for missions. That is why the average modern Christian who reads William Carey's *An Enquiry into the Obligations of Christians, to use Means for the Conversion of the Heathens* would wonder why Carey takes such pains to establish the need for obedience to the Great Commission. We have grown up in a period when mission and our Lord's commission have been regarded as synonymous. Carey, however, wrote at a time when the dominating theological position had almost stifled the missionary zeal of the church. The Great Commission was relegated to the background and seen as binding only on the disciples. The teaching of the Reformers, Calvin and Luther, was that the pastor had no commission to preach to the world but only to take care of his own particular church. Missiology was almost totally absent in the Reformed understanding of ecclesiology.

The church thus received no motivation to reach out in missionary activity. New churches were formed by the dispersion of Christians. William Carey, nurtured in ultra-Calvinistic circles in England, had been influenced by his friend Andrew Fuller and his book *The Gospel Worthy of All Acceptation*. Fuller's stress on the duty of all Christians everywhere to preach the gospel captured Carey's attention. He saw clearly that the duty of all to preach the gospel had been obscured by the Reformers' thinking. His powerful plea and his own efforts to obey the commission ushered in the era of modern missions which resulted in the phenomenal, worldwide spread of Christianity.

Undoubtedly, if we had to point to one passage that would be the driving force of this movement it would be the Great Commission. Carey carefully outlined and emphasized the commission and called his readers to a right response. In our era we have unquestioningly accepted its centrality. Harry R. Boer recently pointed out, however, that a closer look at the biblical account of the life and witness of the early church surprisingly reveals a total absence of any reference to this commission. He showed that it is Pentecost, the outpouring of the Spirit on the church, that appears as the chief factor in the missionary thought and action of the early church.[6]

Roland Allen, ahead of his time, referred to the Spirit who impelled the missionary work of the early church as 'a missionary Spirit.'[7]

> Our conception of the work of the Holy Spirit has been almost confined to the revelation of truth, of holiness, of church government and order. Missionary work as an expression of the Holy Spirit has received such slight and casual attention that it might almost escape the notice of a hasty reader.[8]

We must be careful to point out that Allen, however, makes a distinction between the 'Spirit given at Pentecost' and 'the Spirit which inspired the prophets'.[9] He claims that the

New Testament Spirit is distinct from the Old Testament Spirit, 'the Spirit of the Son, the Spirit of the mission of the Son, the Spirit of the incarnation, the Spirit of redeeming love'.[10] We shall deal with this relationship later in this chapter, taking the position that the Spirit of the Old Testament and the Spirit of the New are one and the same.

In dealing with the role of the Holy Spirit in the mission of the early church, we shall consider some powerful arguments in order to appreciate fully the crucial fact which, surprisingly, the present-day church has overlooked. It could come as a shock to learn that the early church hardly appeals to the Great Commission. Peter speaks of the Gentiles hearing the gospel on the basis of the revelation of God and the universal availability of the Holy Spirit (Acts 15:7–8). Paul refers back only to the command he had received personally (Acts 22:21; 26:16–18; Gal. 1:11–12; Eph. 3:7–8). Let us look at three particular arguments which underline Boer's thesis.

Peter and the Great Commission

The book of Acts records six utterances of Peter that refer to the universality of the gospel.[11] It is clear from these that although there is no doubt in Peter's mind that the gospel has universal implications, he is not explicit about the motivation he derives from the Great Commission. And if we see Acts 10:42, 'He commanded us to preach to the people (*laos*),' as an exception that could contain an implicit reference to the Great Commission, we are faced with a problem. The word *laos* in Lucan usage refers to 'the people of God', in contrast to *ochlos*, the word Luke utilizes for non-Jewish people. Is Peter then restricting the universality of the gospel in the sense that only all the Jews are to receive it? Peter's Jewish exclusivism and particularism cannot be concealed. God, however, deals with him, starting with his powerful experience at Pentecost and later through the vision in Acts 11. Peter comes to understand that God is impartial, and confesses, 'Who was I to think that I could oppose God?' (Acts 11:17). Even if the Great Commission had previously made an impact on him, the Jewishness in him had probably brushed it aside until a more powerful reminder came. He continued to battle with the fact that truly God's gift was to the Gentiles as well as to the Jews (Gal. 2:11–12).

The early church and the Great Commission

The Council of Jerusalem arrived at the conclusion: 'God has granted even the Gentiles repentance unto life' (Acts 11:18). Again, it is surprising that there is no reference back to the Great Commission and our Lord's command to make the gospel universally available. It is even more surprising that Luke, having recorded this acceptance of Gentile participation, proceeds to describe the expansion of the church with no reference to the Great Commission. One can appreciate that Paul's reference point was his own experience and the Lord's personal command, and also Barnabas' work among the Gentiles, since he was not present with the disciples when they received the commission. But we have to accept that the Great Commission plays no explicit part in the mission of the early church. Could it be that the Lord gave no such command after all, as some would argue?

Paul and the Great Commission

Luke emphatically indicates that Paul's motivation came not from the Great Commission but from direct divine intervention. The first indication of Paul's missionary involvement comes in the Lord's words to Ananias: 'Go! This man is my chosen instrument to carry my name before the Gentiles and their kings and before the people of Israel' (9:15). The Holy Spirit then commissions Paul and Barnabas to go out in mission (13:1–3). The first of Paul's recorded statements about his mission to the Gentiles comes in Acts 13:46–47. He points to the Jewish rejection of the message as a reason for turning to the Gentiles. It is not the Great

Commission to which he appeals, but a quotation from Isaiah, pointing out that the apostles are a 'light to the Gentiles' (Is. 49:6).

Later, Paul claims that what God revealed to him was that he would be a witness to all (Acts 22:15). In his defence before Agrippa, too, it is words that Christ spoke to him directly to which he appeals (Acts 26:15–18). In Paul's assertion about his apostleship and his declaration of his missionary calling there is hardly any reference to the Great Commission. Where, then, is the justification for so strong an emphasis today on a command to which even the early church did not look for direction? Could it be that we have blown up out of proportion what the disciples themselves wanted to keep in the background?

Pentecost and the early church

Boer himself is careful not to displace the Great Commission from what he states is 'the heart and soul of all missionary witness'.[12] He wants, however, to show that the commission derives its meaning and power wholly and exclusively from the Pentecost event. We must first outline the significance of this event for the early church.

Peter is the first to refer to the eschatological significance of the event in his speech on the day of Pentecost (2:14–39). The continuity between the Old Testament and the New is clearly established. Pentecost fulfils the Old Testament prophecies about the coming of the Spirit. We can even go right back to the Abrahamic covenant and the promise of blessing to *all* the families of the earth (Gn. 12:3). Boer concludes that 'after creation and incarnation the outpouring of the Spirit is the third great work of God'.[13] Further,

> At Pentecost the Holy Spirit made the church as body of Christ his dwelling place. In distinction from the limiting of his operations to Israel in the old covenant, and from concentration in the Messiah in the Gospels, he became, after Pentecost,

universal in his activities. The church, moreover, became consciously aware of the presence of the Spirit in her midst, and lives and acts in his power. The change that Pentecost effected in the relations of the Spirit to men was therefore radical.[14]

The coming of the Spirit links all the events that make up the total redemptive plan of God, giving continuity between the Old and New Testaments. We have emphasized the need to think of mission in the total perspective of God's dealings with humankind, and the role of the Holy Spirit could be seen as holding this totality together. The forward look of the Old Testament saints is fulfilled in the coming of the Spirit. Although in both the Old and New Testaments the activity of the Holy Spirit is spoken of as a present activity, Pentecost is the arrival of the final dimension in the activity of God in history. Joel 2:28 and Ezekiel 11:19 and 37:14 all look ahead to this event. Jesus too looked ahead to the Holy Spirit's coming (Lk. 24:49; 16:7, 13–14). In fact, the disciples were commanded to 'stay in the city' (Jerusalem) till they had received power from the Holy Spirit (Lk. 24:49; *cf.* Acts 1:4). It is true that John said during Jesus' ministry, 'Up to that time the Spirit had not yet been given' (Jn. 7:39). But this certainly cannot be taken to mean that John was ignorant of the Spirit's activity previously. The explanation must be that John's reference here is to Pentecost and the universal availability and activity of the Holy Spirit. Attempts to establish a discontinuity between the activity of the Spirit in the Old Testament and in the New do no justice to the fact that the apostles accepted only one Spirit. The Spirit who was active in the Old Testament was now poured out in the new covenant of God. What was denied to the people of God in the old covenant has been bestowed on the people of God in the new covenant.

At Pentecost, the activity of the Spirit in the last days was introduced and demonstrated to the church. The individual experience of Pentecost has received so much emphasis that its ecclesiological and eschatological significance has been minimized. Pentecost means that the mission of God is now universal; salvation is for everyone who calls on the name of the Lord (Acts 2:21). God's set purposes for his creation are now available for all. 'The promise is for you and your children and for all who are far off – for all whom the Lord our God will call' (Acts 2:39).

In eschatological language, we have entered into the new and final aeon, which will culminate in the total victory of the Spirit of God over all that belongs to the old age. The Spirit has introduced us already to the anticipation of this glorious life, but we are still in the process of experiencing the final victory. Boer writes of the 'incompatible conjunction or co-existence of the old aeon moving to its consumation'.[15] Even creation groans as it waits for this final redemption (Rom. 8:22).

Grasping the significance of the overlapping of these two aeons restores a New Testament thrust to our mission today. The individual struggle for sanctification, the battle of the church for unity, the groaning of creation for redemption, and all other conflicts, are central to the mission of God to humankind. The restoration brought by the Spirit is not for individuals in isolation from the rest of humanity and history. In the totality of God's purposes, he sends the Spirit to empower the church for its mission. Through him the church declares to the world what is to come by demonstrating even now what has already been done in those who have become his children.

Pentecost or Great Commission?

Boer's thesis, with its thoroughly biblical investigation, leaves us wondering whether we have mistakenly focused attention on the Great Commission instead of on Pentecost. He himself is careful not to dethrone what he believes 'has always been, is now and always will be, the heart and soul of all true missionary labour'. He suggests that the meaning and position of the Great Commission must be construed in a new and different way. While we desire, with Boer, to tread carefully, the question arises whether we have succumbed to a legalistic motivation for mission.

Boer correctly points out that there is an essential link between the Great Commission and the Holy Spirit. Pentecost enables God's people to live in line with God's law. The law has been emphasized so heavily, however, that the Spirit's empowering for mission has received insufficient stress. We need to emphasize the role of the Spirit anew, and to seek to understand within this context Jesus' promise that his disciples would receive power, after which they 'will be my witnesses' (Acts 1:8). This tells us not merely what the church would do, but what the church would be.

The Spirit at Pentecost makes the fear-filled band of disciples into a power-filled, witnessing church. Once the emphasis is placed on what the people of God have become, the mission of God can be seen in its proper perspective. It is the becoming, and not the doing, that makes them the people God wants them to be.

What the church should do in regard to obedience to the law today could be interpreted in terms of action according to a programme, proclaiming Christ in neatly packaged presentations, with even the results systematically predicted. One wonders whether the over-emphasis on this kind of mission has resulted in the mammoth multinational strategies which lack sensitivity to what the Spirit impels us to become in our individual contexts. What the church should be today, as the Spirit empowers it to witness faithfully, should surely be more in keeping with the activity of the early church. Led by the Spirit, the church waited when it needed to wait, prayed when it needed to pray, and acted when it needed to act.

There is a note of spontaneity that comes, not from compulsion to obey a law, but from being faithful to what the Spirit leads us into in each particular situation. The spontaneity of the witness of the early church is captured, for instance, in Peter's words: 'We cannot help speaking about what we have seen and heard' (Acts 4:20). Similarly, Paul declares: 'I am compelled to preach. Woe to me if I do not preach the gospel!' (1 Cor. 9:16). Although there is no reference here to any law, however, we must avoid suggesting that the command of Christ was not in their minds at all.

The role of the Holy Spirit was to bring all of the teaching of Jesus Christ before them – all that was needed to make them a dynamic witness. We cannot maintain that their only motivation was the Great Commission. In fact, according to the Acts of the Apostles, it does not play an obvious part in their motivation. This is significant for mission today, which needs to be clothed afresh with the Spirit of God. Our modern lack of stress on an inner compulsion and on the spontaneity of the work of a God who is far beyond human comprehension is glaring.

Boer is perhaps too careful about upsetting the traditionally accepted view, yet he is bold enough to point to our 'spiritual decadence in so far as the emphasis is on the binding character of the Great Commission and the responsibilities to the Law'.[16] Where the spontaneity of an inner motivation is lacking, activity in obedience to a law can only be an empty engagement. We must, however, admit that the missionary movement, since William Carey reminded the church of the binding character of the Great Commission, has resulted in an unparalleled growth of the Christian community. This does not necessarily justify the place accorded to the Great Commission, but it reminds us of the grace of God that works despite our limitations.

The great need today is for a restoration of a fuller perspective on God's activity in terms of his mission of the kingdom. We have become caught up in trying to put together all the pieces to make up the whole rather than in attempting to grasp the whole itself. If we see that both the Great Commission and Pentecost belong to the one whole redemptive mission of God, we will realize that the one cannot be separated from the other. The 'why' of missions should be the Great Commission and all the other commands of the Lord to become his witnesses in his world. But the 'how' will always be the pentecostal power made available by the Holy Spirit. Further, the 'what' of mission is the cross and resurrection. We cannot separate these elements, but should appreciate that they belong together inseparably in the one kingdom mission in which God has called us to be involved.

A fresh power is needed in mission today. It will not come from reaffirming any command, or from wordy formulations of our commitment to the task, but wholly through the Holy Spirit. The law has no life unless the Spirit activates it. This is not to disparage the law; indeed, the weakness of the church today is partly due to antinomianism. Yet we must avoid being subjected to the law alone. Rather, we should submit to Jesus Christ, our Master. As Roland Allen reminded us: 'Others direct from without, Christ directs within; others order, Christ gives the Spirit who desires and strives for that which he commands; others administer a dead letter, Christ imparts life.'[17]

The Holy Spirit and the ministry of Jesus

We can emphasize the role of the Holy Spirit further when we see the close link between his ministry and that of Jesus Christ. At critical events in the life and ministry of Jesus, the Holy Spirit's activity is so clearly instrumental in accomplishing God's purposes that it cannot be ignored. It is important to underline this close connection, because it demonstrates that the ministry of the Spirit is not different from or contradictory to the ministry of Jesus. Moreover, since Jesus himself needed the Spirit's empowering for his mission, how much more do we need it when seeking to be involved in Jesus' mission.

We can trace the Spirit's activity in Jesus' birth, baptism, temptation and public ministry.

The virgin birth

Matthew and Luke explicitly show that it was through the Holy Spirit that the virgin Mary conceived. 'The Holy Spirit will come upon you,' Luke records (Lk. 1:35), and Joseph finds her 'to be with child through the Holy Spirit' even before they came together (Mt. 1:18). Hindu mythology portrays crude scenes of gods mating with humans to produce offspring, but the biblical narratives depict the Holy Spirit's activity carefully and with dignity. It is unlikely that Luke was using a euphemism for sexual intercourse; rather, he emphasizes the certainty of the hand of God on Mary.

Throughout the Bible the Holy Spirit is seen as the giver of life. The Spirit who acts in creation, the life-giving Spirit, is the one who manifests divine life to dying humanity at the incarnation. The emphasis in the birth narratives is not on the manner in which conception takes place, but primarily on the agency of this conception. The Holy Spirit's activity right from the incarnation could well be seen as God's announcement that the whole mission and ministry of our Lord are to be intimately interwoven with the ministry of the Holy Spirit.

This has obvious implications for the life-giving mission that we are to be involved in as we share the message of the Lord Jesus Christ. When life itself is the content of the message we offer, we should not settle for anything less than fulness of life, and not merely in its spiritual aspect. Because the kingdom mission of God is to restore life in all its aspects, we need to explore ways of working this out in our mission. Led and empowered by the Holy Spirit, the Lord Jesus accomplished his mission. This same Spirit gives life to the church today, enabling it to fulfil its mission.

Jesus' baptism

Significantly, the inaugural event in the ministry of Jesus commands the attention of all the gospel writers. The Spirit's role in the public introduction of Jesus' messianic mission is crucial, as it serves as a divine seal upon it. It is not that Jesus became Messiah at this point; rather, it is here that this office is made public.

So crucial is the activity of the Holy Spirit in the baptism of Jesus that the Spirit's descent is dramatized by the imagery of the dove. Whether the dove is literal or figurative is outside our scope, but what is certain is that the appointing of Jesus to this messianic office is witnessed by all present. This is further attested by the words of the Father, who affirms that Jesus is 'my Son, whom I love; with you I am well pleased' (Lk. 3:22).

The mission of Jesus is not only Spirit-initiated but also Spirit-oriented. The Holy Spirit has already been active in Jesus' life, in his conception as well as in his physical and spiritual growth, but now the world is ready to witness the intimate link between the Spirit and Jesus in fulfilling the mission of God. The same Spirit through whom he was conceived, and through whom he is now baptized and anointed, will equip Jesus to demonstrate the power of God through his authoritative proclamation of the good news, his mighty miraculous works, his atoning death, and his resurrection and exaltation.

Jesus' temptation

Although his baptism is the inaugural event in the ministry of Jesus, it is not till after the temptation that we actually see the commencement of his public ministry. It is perhaps this close link between the baptism and the temptation that makes Mark place the two events in immediate sequence, with an accent on the Holy Spirit playing the dominant role in both. Jesus experiences 'the Spirit descending upon him', the voice from heaven attests his sonship, and 'at once the Spirit sent him out into the desert' to be tempted (Mk. 1:10–13).

Jesus is engaged in a spiritual conflict in which the Spirit leads him to a triumphant encounter. His victory over the devil in the temptation account is only the start of a series of authoritative victories over the demons he will meet in the course of his public ministry. Those who doubt the validity of Jesus' authority over them should take a look at ministries in Asia today. Spirit-filled Christians in similar conflicts make demons shudder and flee at the authoritative name of Jesus. It is sad that some Christians have demythologized mission in their aversion to certain pentecostal and charismatic over-emphases. One of the central characteristics of

Jesus' mission is his victory over Satan, and mission today must continue to confront demonic activities in all their manifestations.[18]

Jesus' public ministry

It is appropriate to start with Luke's account of Jesus' public ministry, for he places the promise of the Spirit in Isaiah 61:1–2 at its outset. Luke undoubtedly reflects the significance of the Spirit's role in the Old Testament expectations of the Messiah. Against that background, we now see that the Old Testament expectations of the Messiah were to be fulfilled in our Lord Jesus, and this is the purpose for which he is anointed by the Spirit. Once again we see the Spirit bringing to God's mission the continuity which is so essential to capturing the impact of the totality of mission as depicted in the Bible.

The references to the filling of the Holy Spirit prior to the temptation (Lk. 4:1), the empowering of the Spirit following the temptation (Lk. 4:14), and the anointing of the Spirit at the commencement of his mission, clearly serve to emphasize the link between the Holy Spirit and Jesus Christ in the messianic mission. From now on, the Spirit will work in and through Jesus Christ, the anointed one, to accomplish God's purposes. The stress on this link underlines the continuing role of the Holy Spirit in the mission of the church today. Is this not what Jesus emphasized in his Paraclete discourses (Jn. 15:26–16:15)?

Just as Jesus' ministry commenced only after he had been filled, empowered and anointed by the Holy Spirit, so the disciples are told not to embark on their ministry until the Spirit has come upon them. They must wait (Lk. 24:49). When they were empowered at Pentecost, they would commence a witness with the potential to reach the ends of the earth (Acts 1:8). The Spirit, then, is central not only to the public ministry of Jesus, but also to the continuation of this ministry through his followers, his church, who, like Jesus, must be led by the Spirit.

The Holy Spirit and individuals

Our stress on the role of the Holy Spirit in the church's life and witness is not meant to depreciate the ministry of the Spirit in the individual's life. But we must clarify the point made elsewhere about the over-emphasis on the individualized gospel. This should not be taken to mean that there is no place for the individual in mission. This section on the role of the Holy Spirit in the individual should help to avoid any misunderstanding.

Individual salvation

Before he left this world, Jesus said, 'I am going to send you what my Father has promised.' His disciples would be 'clothed with power from on high' (Lk. 24:49). Pentecost witnessed the clothing and ushered in the community of those who would be called 'Christians'. This community would comprise individual men and women saved 'in Christ' through the activity of the Holy Spirit. This Spirit initiates conviction of sin (Jn. 16:8), sets us apart for obedience to Christ (1 Pet. 1:2), enables us to call Jesus our Lord (1 Cor. 12:3), and assures us that we are children of God (Rom. 8:9b, 14–17). The ministry of applying these redemptive benefits to the church belongs to the Holy Spirit, who performs in each person the miracle of God's grace made available through Christ.

Regeneration

Nicodemus, steeped in his religion, struggled to understand the thrust of Jesus' teaching that 'no-one can enter the kingdom of God unless he is born of water and the Spirit' (Jn. 3:5). Put plainly, flesh gives birth to flesh and spirit gives birth to spirit. Nicodemus was certainly getting more than he bargained for! Even this Pharisee, this member of the Jewish ruling council, despite all his prominence, needed to be 'born of the Spirit'. Being 'born anew' or 'born from above' is not the result of human effort, as is sometimes erroneously communicated in our evangelistic mission. It is God's initiative, brought about by the Holy Spirit.

Humanity in its fallen condition contrasts with Christ in his Spirit-filled condition. We cannot make right choices (Rom. 1:32), cannot accept the things that come from the Spirit of God (1 Cor. 2:14), cannot please God (Rom. 8:8), and cannot accept God (Jn. 14:17). There is no way we can set our own lives right. God, therefore, has given the Spirit to initiate a response in us towards God. The Holy Spirit, who lifts us from our fallenness, gives us new life in Christ, in whom we live as children of God, experiencing the reality of being born anew.

While we must avoid communicating this message in a way that Hindus might misunderstand, there is no need to discard the concept of the new birth. The Hindu, in his desire to break out of the cycle of birth and death, is in fact seeking how *not* to be born again. Possible misunderstandings arise from the way in which the term 'born again' has become identified with present-day gospel preaching. Jesus' emphasis is on a birth from above, a new birth, and this every Hindu will readily accept.

Adoption

Those of us who preach the message in Asia usually confront impersonal relationships in religious experience. Once again, the personal nature of God brings us into the richness of a personal relationship. 'How great is the love the Father has lavished on us!' (1 Jn. 3:1), having through the Spirit made us his children. The graphic metaphor of adoption brings out the personal character of this relationship we enjoy with God through the Spirit (Rom. 8:14–17; Gal. 4:6). Not only the richness but also the intimacy of this relationship stirs us, bringing us into '*Abba*' terms with our heavenly Father. Not only that, we are now co-heirs with Christ (Rom. 8:17). All of the Spirit that was available to Jesus is now available to us, since we receive all things with him (Rom. 8:32).

Two aspects of the work of the Spirit in relation to adoption need to be considered. First, in Christ a person 'is no longer a slave, but a son' (Gal. 4:7). This is an accomplished reality for those who are 'led by the Spirit' (Rom. 8:14), for we have not received a spirit that makes us a slave to fear, but rather have received 'the Spirit of sonship' (Rom. 8:15). It is a present possession to which 'the Spirit himself testifies' (Rom. 8:16), and therefore an assured relationship. Because people often turn to God initially through fear and superstition, we need to underline this fact of adoption in order to lead the believer into a more meaningful relationship with God.

There is, however, also a sense in which this adoption is yet to be fully realized. Paul says that even we, 'who have the firstfruits of the Spirit, groan inwardly as we wait eagerly for our adoption as sons, the redemption of our bodies' (Rom. 8:23). He implies that although we enjoy the firstfruits now, the full benefits of the harvest will come only through this same Spirit in the future. John puts it vividly when he says that 'now we are the children of God, and what we will be has not yet been made known' (1 Jn. 3:2). We continue with this theme as we turn to the Spirit's role in assurance.

Assurance

The Holy Spirit is described as 'a deposit guaranteeing our inheritance until the redemption of those who are God's possession' (Eph. 1:14). This role of the Spirit in assuring us of our position as well as our possession in Christ is portrayed through several Pauline metaphors.

First, we have the Pauline word 'firstfruits', familiar to the farmer who judges the quality of the final crop on the basis of the first of the harvest. If the firstfruits are good, the final crop will be good. The Holy Spirit as the 'firstfruits' would be better appreciated if the church were to provide more teaching on the Spirit. There are some congregations where any reference to the Holy Spirit is avoided lest they be branded 'pentecostal'. Yet the church was brought into being and is held together by his activity. We are sustained by God's Word, and inspired and illuminated by the Holy Spirit. If this is merely the first-fruits, the final harvest will surely be beyond all our human expectations.

Secondly, we have the word 'seal' from the world of commerce. Paul reminds the Ephesian Christians that when they believed they 'were marked in him with a seal, the promised Holy Spirit' (Eph. 1:13). The seal on an article was stamped with its owner's mark. The seal of the Holy Spirit thus identifies us as children of God, having tasted of Christ's salvation. Sadly, we have too often been marked by organizational identities, internal political squabbles, materialistic preoccupations and high-powered business infrastructures which have been more visible than this seal. It is time we allowed the Holy Spirit to burn away that false exterior and make our identity more recognizable.

Paul employs another commercial word when he describes the Holy Spirit as a 'deposit' or 'earnest' (AV) who guarantees complete payment or possession (Eph. 1:14). 'It is God who has . . . given us the Spirit as a deposit, guaranteeing what is to come.' The first instalment or down-payment secures the transaction. The Holy Spirit is this guarantee, assuring us of the full salvation that we will one day enjoy in Christ.

To these three Pauline pictures we may add a fourth, the highly debated Johannine term 'Paraclete', which further stresses God's assurance of Christ's presence with us. We are not concerned here with the meaning of the word, but with the fact that Jesus refers to the Holy Spirit as *'another* Paraclete'. In other words, the Holy Spirit would be to the disciples what Jesus Christ had already been to them. Jesus was soon to leave his disciples, but during his absence the Holy Spirit would continue to assure them of Christ's presence and of his eventual triumphant return to receive his church into glory. Jesus' work was not to cease at his death and resurrection, nor was his fellowship with his disciples to terminate upon his departure from them.

The misleading invitation in our gospel message, 'Accept Christ into your heart,' needs to be corrected. The biblical picture is of a filling by the Spirit of God who brings the presence of Christ to the believer. There is, however, a continuity between the Spirit and Jesus in Jesus' statement: 'I will not leave you as orphans; I will come to you' (Jn. 14:18). Again, all that Jesus was to his disciples will now be represented to those same disciples, and to the church soon to take birth, by the Spirit. The believer needs no greater assurance than that of the indwelling Holy Spirit, the Paraclete who continues to guarantee our present and future redemption in Christ.

The Holy Spirit and the mission of the individual

One consequence of understanding the intricate link between the Holy Spirit and mission is that it enables us to appreciate the full, God-intended dimensions of mission, which are far wider than a mere church programme. If the Christian's entire life is seen as being controlled by the Holy Spirit, he is able to see that in fact the outworking of this life is itself mission. This view gives mission a true wholeness, which contrasts with the artificially strung-together elements which we often portray as 'mission'. When the Holy Spirit becomes central, controlling, directing, establishing priorities and enabling, we shall witness a natural, or rather supernatural, wholeness in mission.

The emphasis in this approach to mission is, first, more on our being available to God than on doing what we think is important for God. Bishop John Taylor says that 'the gift of the Holy Spirit in the fellowship of the church first enables Christians to be and only as a consequence of that sends them to do and to speak'.[19] The consequence of putting the primary emphasis on preaching or on serving, he points out, is to erect 'a functional barrier between ourselves and our fellow humans, casting ourselves in a different role from the rest of men'.[20] The Holy Spirit must be allowed to make us more human, so that we can truly manifest the wholeness in mission that God desires.

Secondly, this approach to mission restores the spontaneity the church so urgently needs to refresh its life and witness. The depressed and defeated disciples, much against their human inclination, awaited the outpouring of the Holy Spirit whom God had promised. True to his word, God filled them. And from then on there was a spontaneity in mission that made the small, insignificant group turn the then known world upside down.

The Holy Spirit not only motivates but also empowers people to set out on their God-given mission. This spontaneity leads them to confess, 'We cannot help speaking about what we have seen and heard' (Acts 4:20). Restoring such an attitude should not be taken to condone a lack of planning, discipline and orderliness in mission. These are characteristics of the Holy Spirit and must not be sacrificed. Nevertheless, we need to seek afresh the touch of the Spirit so that the church today may fulfil its mission with fresh zeal.

The Holy Spirit and the church

We have underlined the fact that the life and dynamic of the church begin only with the descent of the Holy Spirit who empowers it to be the agent of God's mission. The people of God brought together by the Holy Spirit are a people united in a common mission. 'This great work of the Spirit is called the church.'[21] The church, then, owes its existence to the Spirit, as Paul implies when he says that we are being 'built together to become a dwelling in which God lives by his Spirit' (Eph. 2:22).

George Smeaton cautions against the one-sided emphasis that sees the church as emanating from the 'Spirit's own proper motion'.[22]

> An analogy may be traced between the baptism of
> Christ, by which he was inaugurated into office,

and the effusion of the Spirit on the day of Pentecost, after he received the plenary unction of the Spirit (Acts 2:33). In a word, these two events indicated two grades of unction, or two stages in the communication of the Spirit to him. The former, accompanied by the descent of the Spirit, was meant to equip the Redeemer for entering his office. The latter was intended to found the Christian church and supply it with the living organs and various gifts by which it efficiently exercises the spiritual life for the advancement of the Christian cause.[23]

This again points to the link between the Spirit and Jesus Christ which we have already seen.

Having experienced this filling, the church is not left to itself to conduct the mission entrusted to it by Jesus Christ. It is to be continually 'filled with the Spirit' (Eph. 5:18), to fight with the sword of the Spirit (Eph. 6:17), to 'pray in the Spirit on all occasions' (Eph. 6:18), and above all to 'live by the Spirit' (Gal. 5:16). The church, as a witness to the indwelling Spirit, should, moreover, bring forth the 'fruit of the Spirit' (Gal. 5:22–23). Peter refers to God's elect as 'chosen according to the foreknowledge of God the Father, through the sanctifying work of the Spirit' (1 Pet. 1:2).

The church cannot but depend on the Spirit for its mission. The long-accepted division between the local church and the mission agencies is artificial and unwarranted. It is the church that must be involved in mission. This does not mean that there is no longer room for parachurch agencies. Yet we need to take a fresh look at ecclesiology, refusing to restrict the meaning of the church in narrow, denominational terms, but embracing its broadest missiological significance within the kingdom of God. Only then will the church be recognized as fulfilling its rightful role as a Spirit-initiated church on the Spirit-motivated mission of the kingdom of God.

PART 3

Contemporary Christian mission

10

The church and God's mission today

Our discussion of biblical themes and contextual issues relating to mission has brought us to the point where we can draw out some important implications of God's mission to the world through his church. There are three main reasons for emphasizing the central role of the church. First, the church's centrality in God's mission has been disregarded, and that needs to be addressed. Secondly, too many recent mission activities have been conducted merely by individuals or organizations with no reference to the church, and this needs to be corrected. Thirdly, and even more importantly, the church as the people of God has not been faithfully involved in the mission of God's kingdom. Over the years it has become caught up in internal activities, and its thrust within the world, where it is supposed to be God's witness, has diminished.

This concluding chapter will discuss three major concerns. First, the church needs to discover its missiological essence. Mission is not something forced on it from outside, but something that belongs to the church's very nature. Secondly, the church must underline the uniqueness of its message. Only when we are convinced of the unique importance of the revelation of Jesus Christ in the salvation of the world we will be convinced that mission is necessary. Thirdly, the church needs to discover the totality of God's mission.

The church's missionary character

Having considered the nature and the function of the

people called together to display the glory of their God, we shall by now have no doubt that we today have missed out on the very essence of the church. Right from the time of the Reformation, attempts have been made to understand the church biblically. Calvin wrote in his *Institutes*: 'Whenever we see the word of God sincerely preached and heard, wherever we see the sacraments administered according to the institution of Christ, there we cannot have any doubts that the church of God has some existence.'[1] Where the word is preached faithfully and where the sacraments are administered, there is the church.

Calvin, like Luther, was fighting against the institutionalized understanding of the Roman Church. Luther reduced the marks of the church to just one – the preaching of the word. The church is pure, Luther claimed, where the pure gospel is preached. 'The church does not make the word but it comes into being from the word.'[2]

However much the Reformers tried to get away from the institutional idea of the church, all that they wrote has primarily to do with the nature of the church. Not much is said about the church's mission to the world. The urgent need today is to discover the biblical essence of the church, which will point to a spontaneity in its mission, something that is embedded in the very heart of its being. The church's twofold dynamic – worship and witness – must be fully explored so that mission finds an integral place in its life and witness.

Ecclesiology without missiology

The church without mission, ecclesiology without missiology, is only a static symbol of what God wants his living body to be in its witness to the world today. Despite the Reformers' achievement in establishing the true nature of the church in its christocentricity and in its relationship to the preached Word, they failed to get to the heart of God's concern for mission. The Roman Catholic Church was far more missionary-minded. A Roman Catholic polemicist wrote: 'The Lutherans compare themselves to the apostles and the evangelists, yet they have ... hardly converted even so much as a handful.'[3] We must be careful not to conclude that the preaching of the gospel throughout the world was foreign to Luther's thought, but it is obvious that mission plays no central part in the life of the church as he understood it. There was therefore almost no attempt by Protestants to propagate the faith outside Europe.

For the Reformers, the work of missions required a special office – one that either had already been fulfilled by the preaching of the apostles or which rested solely with the sovereignty of God who acted in whatever way was needed at a particular time. For example, Luther held that the offices of apostle, prophet and evangelist were extraordinary. 'They were not instituted in the church to be perpetual but only to endure so long as churches were to be formed where none previously existed.'[4] In other words, while God from time to time would raise up men to fulfil these functions, the sending forth of missionaries or evangelists was not an essential part of the church's ministry.

Similarly, although Luther stressed the individual's responsibility to preach and teach the gospel to non-Christians, based on the doctrine of the priesthood of all believers, the motive was not any missionary mandate to the church, but simply brotherly love. The failure to weave a biblical missiology into the fabric of our ecclesiology naturally results in an ineffective and incomplete church with only a partial understanding of its nature and function.

This absence of a concept of mission and of the missionary obligation of the church developed into a theological prejudice that hindered missionary activity in the post-Reformation period. It was a reaction to this attitude that stirred William Carey and eventually brought men and women together for Edinburgh 1910. There was a deep consciousness of the need to renew the church and to call it to take its missionary role seriously. But the growing phenomenon of foreign-mission societies and boards, which were supported only by individuals in the church, began to raise problems. The missionary movement was pleading with the church to accept its own essential missionary character. But the church was still caught up in ecclesiastical politics, preoccupied with sustaining its own existence.

Lessons from history must be heeded, and the church today must develop a proper biblical ecclesiology which would give missiology its rightful place. Our discussion of biblical themes relevant to mission, starting from creation, has underlined the importance of God's total plan that has been worked out through his historical acts and is now being manifested through his church – a people in worship and witness. Unless this dynamic is discovered from within, no amount of challenge from outside will arouse the church to fulfil its role in God's plans for his kingdom.

Churches have always been caught up with their own survival and have hardly recognized the priority of reaching out. In fact, such a reaching out could well have seemed a threat to their survival. A Chinese delegate to Edinburgh expressed his longing for a 'united Christian church without any denominational distinctions'.[5] The church, caught up in its own denominational survival, stifles the missionary concern that is so vital to its existence. These attitudes pointed firmly to the need for a proper biblical ecclesiology which would give missiology its rightful place.

Missiology without ecclesiology

While an ecclesiology without missiology hinders mission, missiology unrelated to ecclesiology is an equally grave concern. We have seen how mission was reconceptualized in the belief that God's primary relationship was to the world, and not to the church and then to the world. The traditional God–church–world sequence was said to be outdated, and the God–world–church sequence was seen as the direction of mission today. The church was being sidelined. This amounted to an understanding of God's mission without any emphasis on the church – missiology without ecclesiology.

The Bible is clear on the central role the church is to play in mission. The mission of Israel gives us ample evidence that it is God's people whom he wants to use in his purposes. In his electing Israel, God established that he would work through a particular group of people to reveal his mission to the whole world. Israel anticipated the role of the church, and today it is this body that carries responsibility for God's kingdom mission. While we have emphasized that there is no church without mission, it is equally important to underline that there is no mission without the church. The two are inextricably bound together.

In the light of this truth, we must note that not only liberal Protestantism, but even the evangelical missionary movement of recent times, are equally to blame for bypassing the church. The present-day phenomenon of the mushrooming of missionary organizations is largely brought about by individuals and groups working outside the church. The label 'parachurch' often reflects not a willingness to get alongside the church and to establish a clear link with it, but a desire to justify activity outside the church.

The balance is to be brought about by giving equal weight to both sides. On the one hand, we need a better understanding of the church, broad enough to see that it is a people in witness as well as a people in worship. We have restricted ourselves to denominational interpretations of the church instead of appreciating the fulness of this body as depicted in the Bible. On the other hand, we need to understand mission as the way the body demonstrates its being in Christ, rather than merely as an activity of the body.

The church-growth movement pioneered by Donald MacGavran has played a significant role in linking mission with the church in recent times. As a result many today are discovering that mission and the church are inseparable, and have turned away from evangelistic movements to church-planting agencies. This new trend has helped to forge the link between church and mission much more strongly. Mission and evangelistic agencies that work on their own, and evangelists who operate alone, need to discover this biblical framework in order to make their ministries fulfilling as part of God's mission through his church today.

The uniqueness of the revelation of Jesus Christ

In addition to the need to give the church a missiological foundation, it is essential that the people of God should affirm the uniqueness of the Christian message. Fervour in mission will be in direct proportion to the church's commitment to the uniqueness of the revelation of Jesus Christ and the conviction that this is the message for the world. The present dilution of the content of mission, and the decline in commitment to mission, is related to the lack of clearcut acceptance of the uniqueness of the message of salvation in Jesus Christ.

The challenge of pluralism

The influential book provokingly entitled *The Myth of Christian Uniqueness*[6] sets out some recent attitudes to this uniqueness. The writers express their desire for a new interpretation, noting that the truth of Christianity lies not on its literal surface but within its ever-changing historical and personal meaning. Their complaint is that 'in much Christian discourse, the "uniqueness of Christianity" has taken on a larger mythological meaning. It has come to signify the unique definitiveness, absoluteness, normativeness and superiority of Christianity in comparison with other religions of the world.'[7] Their intention is to remove this mythological understanding by bringing about a new attitude.

This new understanding seeks to take us beyond the two popular attitudes that have prevailed in relation to other religions: the conservative, exclusivist attitude which accepted that salvation is found only in Christ, and the liberal, inclusivist position which, while recognizing the richness of other faiths, viewed this richness as a result of Christ's redemptive work. What is proposed now is a truly pluralistic position which would recognize the independent validity of all religions. Proponents of this view wish to build three bridges between Christianity and other religions.

The first is the historico-cultural bridge of relativity. This underlines the limitation of all knowledge and religious beliefs, and the difficulty, even the impossibility, of judging other religions on the basis of one's own. John Hick, one of the most ardent proponents, concludes:

> It seems impossible to make the global judgment that any one religious tradition has contributed more good, or less evil, than others. As vast complex totalities, the world traditions seem to be more or less on a par with each other. None can be singled out as manifestly superior.[8]

The second bridge is the theologico-mystical – recognizing the authentic religious experience of mystery in all religions. Mystery demands religious pluralism, and no religion can claim to be the 'only' or the 'final' word. Raimundo Panikkar and Stanley Samartha are the spokesmen for this position, claiming that all religions can participate in and reflect on this mystery, but none can own it.[9] There is no one, universal system that can be imposed on the others. Many systems, with their differences and disagreements, will always exist. We should seek to preserve the uniqueness of all religions.

The third is the ethico-practical bridge, based on the need to promote justice. The proponents of this view see neither historical relativity nor mystery as the key to pluralism. They point to what they see as the exploitative nature of upholding Christianity as the highest revelation and the resulting outrageous and absurd religious chauvinism. The religions of this world should rather share a concern for justice. The strongest case for a pluralistic attitude, runs this argument, is not any need for salvific, revelational, or rational harmony, but the moral and ethical need we face today.

One thing is clear as we read *The Myth of Christian Uniqueness*. We are confronted with a totally different idea of mission. If mission is defined at the start as the pursuit of religious harmony, that is what one will seek to justify. Hick, Knitter and the other contributors are clear on this aim. In scanning the pages of the Bible for a holistic understanding of the church's mission, however, we have discovered that anything less than a presentation of the ultimate claims of Jesus Christ falls far short of the mission entrusted to the church today.

Our commitment to God's mission is genuine only if it is based on a conviction of its uniqueness, finality and decisiveness. The resurgence of religions and the fervency of their missionary zeal results from a belief in the finality of their claims. Most of these claims undermine Christian claims. The devout Hindu or the committed Muslim is not looking for compromise. Why, then, do we emphasize the need for a pluralistic embrace? Anyone who wants to take the biblical claims seriously will see the impossibility of religious passivism. A commitment to the biblical mission demands a commitment to the ultimacy of Jesus Christ, and only when we are thus committed shall we truly see the church set on fire in response to God's call to be involved in his kingdom plans.

The finality of Jesus Christ

It is not just recently that we have begun to be confronted by such calls to compromise Christ's claims; earlier in this book, we traced these forces within the ecumenical movement even before Tambaram 1938. Facing pressure from within as well as without, it is imperative that any biblical theology of mission accentuate the uniqueness of the Christian revelation and confront people with the uncompromising claims of Christ.

Bishop Stephen Neill, in a discussion of this problem, states:

> We must recognize afresh the immense originality of Jesus Christ. Under the influence of 'comparative religion' and similar tendencies we have been too much inclined to find parallels to the works of Jesus here, there and everywhere, and to suppose that he can be fitted into the category of prophet, or genius, or religious leader, or whatever we prefer. But this is simply wrong. Jesus cannot be understood in any dimension other than his own. He has called into being a new world of reality in which only those are at home who call him Lord. When Christians use the word 'God', they mean the Father of our Lord Jesus Christ and nothing else. This is a truth that we forget at our peril.[10]

The point is strongly stated, and our biblical theology must be equally strong if we are effectively to confront people of other religions with the uniqueness of the Christian revelation and the inexorable claims of Christ upon the world. A biblical call for such a confrontation has been brought to our notice by missiological discussions of the role of elenctics. The word 'elenctic' finds its root in the Greek verb *elengchō*, which means 'to rebuke', 'to convict', 'to refute', 'to expose sin'.[11] The verb occurs sixteen times in the New Testament, and the noun twice. Putting together the shades of meaning, an elenctic confrontation can be summed up as 'a confrontation with error in which error is exposed for what it is, the one guilty of error feels rebuked and compelled to admit his error, and, one hopes, is led to repentance'.[12]

Men and women must be confronted with the claims of Christ through an encounter with Christ himself. Error must be exposed and God's desire to bring people to repentance must be passionately made known. The primacy of this proclamation is heavily underlined in the Bible. This task can be fulfilled only when we ourselves are convinced of the uniqueness of God's revelation in Jesus Christ. Jesus is God's final word to humanity. Any belief less than this would dilute the message and minimize the intensity of the biblical mission.

We urgently need to rediscover this proclamation within our context today. Confrontation does not necessarily imply antagonism. That kind of preaching is all too familiar. We need to develop a fresh sensitivity for our context – a new theology of religions, in fact, that will enable us to approach men and women with the compassion of Christ. The kind of confrontation that brings people into an encounter with Christ, seeing their need to respond to the claims of Christ, should not unnecessarily antagonize or build barriers.

The early Christians daringly demonstrated confidence in the finality of God's revelation in Jesus in the face of the prevailing philosophies and ideologies. Yet their sensitivity in dealing with other sincere worshippers or God-fearing Gentiles is something that we need to look at carefully. While it offers us no excuse to relax the claims of Christ on people today, we do need to consider how best to proclaim this same message in the present context of a revival of religious fervour. The kind of pluralistic attitude we are constantly called to demonstrate is certainly in keeping with the mood of our day, but it is far from biblically justifiable. Our missiology must be based on the uniqueness of the biblical revelation, the full and final revelation of God in the Lord Jesus Christ. But it must also be related to our present world.

Understanding the totality of God's mission

In developing a biblical understanding of God's mission,

we have consistently emphasized the need for a total perspective on the mission of God's kingdom. To claim categorically that we can see all the details of this perspective would be presumptuous. This is not what we want to claim. We must recover the thrust of the totality of God's concern in order to see that there is room for the church to express itself fully as the vehicle of God's mission in the world today.

The need for a complete biblical horizon

As we have looked at the Bible afresh, we have been challenged to broaden our horizons to take in the total picture of God's purposes for humanity and its world. We have stressed the biblical whole in order to reveal the limited horizons within which we have worked – whether the individual perspective, the 'evangelism only' perspective, or even the incomplete perspective that arises from basing our missiology simply on the life of Jesus Christ. The value of this total perspective is that it places every aspect of God's mission in its proper position. We must understand the various parts within an integrated whole.

Too often we have operated on the basis of the New Testament picture of mission alone. In searching the Old Testament we have discovered an overall plan within which we constantly need to see Jesus Christ's mission.

Some may disagree that mission has confined its studies to the New Testament, maintaining that we are familiar with systematic treatments of Old Testament themes and their development in the New Testament. Have we not studied the entire plan of redemption as presented throughout the Bible? While we have studied those themes in relation to systematic theology, however, the true missiological potential of this theology has not been properly explored. At the most, missiology has been merely one section of our theology. We are now challenged to see theology as missiological, rather than attempting to touch up missiology with theological paint. Even our brief examination of the Bible's portrayal of the working of God in the world has revealed a missionary God who fulfills missionary purposes. We need to explore this emphasis on missiology in order to make our theology dynamic and contextual.

We do not propose, however, that the whole of theology should be taken over by the missiologists. Far from it. The model of the church as a people in worship and a people in witness is the best model for theology. As a worshipping people, the church stabilizes and strengthens itself. The people of God gather to worship the head of the church, God in Christ. This is the basis of the church's life and functioning. The church must confirm its relationship with its Creator. Similarly, theology too has its own rationale which it must establish. It must act as an aid to the stability and strength of the worshipping church.

As a witnessing people, the church is a body in action, a people on a mission, a worshipping community on a witnessing commission. Worship is not the church's be-all and end-all. The church must go out in response to the command of Christ. Similarly, theology must motivate people to get involved in God's mission. The church that ends with worship alone will be an incomplete church. Similarly, a theology that ends with no more than the edification of students and an increase in their knowledge of God's Word will be an incomplete theology.

Our theology thus needs two dimensions. The first is vertical. We could call it 'doxological', for it has to do with the praise and worship of God. For too long we have approached theology academically instead of being dynamically involved with it. If we look back into church history, we find that theology used to depict the doxological adoration of God. Our academic emphasis has diminished this doxological goal which theology should have. Theology with this dimension will be vibrant and life-giving.

The other dimension is horizontal – the 'missiological' dimension. Theology in its doxological and missiological dimensions will remind the church that it is both a people in worship and a people in witness. It is time theological education was brought into line with this total perspective rather than continuing to adopt fixed and lifeless models.

Yet we are not to restrict our focus to the church. We need, as this book has argued, a kingdom perspective. Our understanding has been limited because our focus has been too narrow. We have looked at mission through denominational spectacles. We need a wider vision which will take in the whole horizon of God's dealings with mankind and its world.

In searching for this complete perspective, we cannot ignore the kingdom goal that the Bible presents for the mission that Jesus Christ has entrusted to his people. And to be faithful to God's mission we need to fit our understanding into this broader whole. Some recent missiological debates have unfortunately consisted of sections of the church attempting to justify their own particular emphasis from their own perspective. Evangelicals have not been isolated from these debates on the meaning and essence of mission. It is vital to recover an understanding of the kingdom horizon so that we shall be able to see the parts within God's whole.

Evangelism and social action

Recent debates on the elements of mission, particularly the prolonged debate over the relationship between evangelism and social action, has mostly consisted of attempting to see how the elements relate to one another within our limited understanding of mission. We have struggled to establish a relationship between the two as though they were foreign to each other. In approaching the relationship from the perspective of the whole, however, we are able to do full biblical justice to each of these elements.

In searching for such a whole, some have argued for the partnership of evangelism and social action within God's mission. At one extreme, some argue that evangelism is the sole component of mission, while at the other, some see mission as wholly social action.[13] Between these two extremes, many today seek some kind of a relationship between evangelism and social action. Few, if any, will deny the need to demonstrate Christian concern in concrete, practical ways, whether they consider this as part of God's mission or not.

Rather than talk about God's mission we should perhaps talk about God's concern, God's kingdom concern. Those willing to explore the potential of this holistic understanding open themselves to the fullest possible involvement in all that God wants for his world and for the people he has created. In this sense, mission, if that is what we insist on calling it, becomes far more than concern about people and society. It must embrace the full range of the concern that a caring God expresses in the outworking of his redemption of his created world.

We have emphasized the fact that proclamation is primary in the witness of the church. It is not, however, the sum total of our life and witness. The gifts given to the church enable it to demonstrate the good news of the kingdom in many and varied ways (Rom. 12:6–8; 1 Cor. 12:4–11; Eph. 4:7–13). It is not enough to proclaim this good news without demonstrating it in concrete ways. The church today must live out its total nature, thus giving a much-needed demonstration of all that God wants it to be. It may not be perfect, but at least some evidence of its true nature ought to be visible to the world.

We all readily accept that making known the kingdom is not a matter of merely announcing it. The time, effort and resources that evangelicals have expended in arguing for and against the necessity of social action or any other element have subtly diverted us from a fully rounded, biblical understanding of proclamation. Must we not demonstrate what we proclaim? Jesus himself held proclamation and demonstration together, and was readily available for whatever God wanted him to do. His being on the kingdom mission led to a spontaneity that is conspicuously lacking in the church's life and mission today, because our understanding is too limited.

Our preoccupation with the elements of mission has led us to seek to forge a partnership between evangelism and social action, implicitly accepting that the two elements are alien. Making known the kingdom of God consists of both proclamation and demonstration, however, and they constitute one whole – mission which is an act of obedience to God's call to *be* rather than simply to *do*. Involvement in the mission of the kingdom does not consist of fulfilling a certain job description and carefully balancing the elements of this mission. Rather, because we are citizens of the kingdom, we are impelled to live the life of the kingdom. Again, this gives rise to the spontaneity of the people of God. Our prime concern is not to hold disparate elements together, or even to maintain priorities in mission, but to submit to God as representatives of his kingdom so that his purposes may be accomplished through the obedience of his people. Mission will be incomplete unless it takes in the whole horizon of the kingdom.

Putting flesh on the gospel

Challenged by biblical insights, we become convinced of the need to demonstrate the gospel in practical ways in responding to this challenge. However, we must beware of artificially forced activities. The practical outworking of the gospel must be seen as integral to the character of the church and its mission. Incarnational mission is a priority. This fleshing out of the gospel makes the message real to the outside world, and spontaneously expresses the kingdom essence of the church. The gospel is actualized.

The question will always be asked: how can we communicate the gospel of the kingdom to a world alien to God's purpose? For the answer we look to Jesus himself, recognizing that he made the kingdom actual in his life and ministry. Speaking with the authority of God, he reminded his hearers that 'the kingdom of God is near you' (Lk. 10:9, 11). We have seen that this means nothing less than the fact that Jesus himself is the kingdom. His nearness to us signifies the nearness of the kingdom, and hence the mission of the kingdom is the mission of Jesus himself. When the church faithfully seeks to follow its Lord closely, its mission is more effective. It is then that the message is made real and actual, and the church is true to its call. This is the true dynamic of the church's mission.

When the gospel is made real, when it is actualized, the relevance of the kingdom message within the church is truly expressed. Only when the message has first been appropriated by the people of God can the church effectively communicate the good news to the world. The emphasis is on the obedience of the church as it surrenders to Jesus Christ, available to be a channel through which God can express his kingdom concern.

We give to the world what we have. When the people of God are charged with the power of Jesus Christ, their words and their deeds speak of the kingdom. Actualizing the gospel, making it real, therefore, is not something external to believers, for they are only living out what they have already experienced. Whether they must speak or act in order to make an impact is not the question.

The message made flesh in the life of the church provides the solid platform from which to proclaim the gospel of the kingdom. This will restore the church's true missionary character and thereby demonstrate the very dynamic of the kingdom. But this will come about only when the church is willing to submit fully to the Lord Jesus Christ, in whom God was pleased to have all his fulness dwell (Col. 1:19). In submitting in this way, the church will discover her part in God's total mission, his kingdom concern 'to reconcile to himself all things, whether things on earth or things in heaven' (Col. 1:20). This is the mission of God's kingdom.

Bibliography

Allen, Roland, *The Ministry of the Spirit* (selected writings, ed. David M. Paton; World Dominion Press, 1960)

Avis, Paul D. L., *The Church in the Theology of the Reformers* (John Knox, 1981)

Barclay, William, *Letters to Philippians, Colossians and Thessalonians* (Saint Andrew Press, 1972)

Bavinck, J. H., *An Introduction to the Science of Missions* (Presbyterian and Reformed, 1960)

The Bible and Theology in Asian Contexts (Asia Theological Association, 1984)

Boer, Harry, R., *Pentecost and Mission* (Eerdmans, 1961)

Brown, Colin (ed.), *The New International Dictionary of the New Testament* (Paternoster, 1971)

Bruce F. F., *The Acts of the Apostles* (IVP, 1965)

— *The Time is Fulfilled* (Eerdmans, 1978)

Calvin, John, *Institutes of the Christian Religion* (1536; Mac-Donald Publishing Co., no date)

Cole, Alan, *Exodus* (Tyndale Old Testament Commentaries; IVP, 1973)

Cotterell, Peter, *The Eleventh Commandment* (IVP, 1981)

Crim, Keith R. (ed.), *The Interpreter's Dictionary of the Bible* (Abingdon, 1979), 4 vols.

Douglas, J. D. (ed.), *The New Bible Dictionary* (IVP, 2nd edn., 1982)

Gadamer, Hans-Georg, *Truth and Method* (Sheed and Ward, 1975)

Gutiérrez, Gustavo, *A Theology of Liberation* (SCM, 1977)

Hedlund, R. E., *Roots of the Great Debate in Mission* (Evangelical Literature Service, 1981)

Hick, John, and Knitter, Paul (eds.), *The Myth of Christian Uniqueness* (Orbis Books, 1988)

Hoekstra, Harvey T., *The World Council of Churches and the Demise of Evangelism* (Tyndale House, 1979)

Horner, N. A. (ed.), *Protestant Crosscurrents in Mission* (Abingdon, 1968)

Jacob, Edmond, *The Theology of the Old Testament* (Hodder and Stoughton, 1958)

Käseman, Ernst, *New Testament Questions of Today* (SCM, 1969)

Kitamori, Kazoh, *Theology of the Pain of God* (SCM, 1958)

Kuriakose, M. K., *History of Christianity in India: Source Materials* (Indian Theological Library no. 9; Serampore University)

Ladd, G. E., *A Theology of the New Testament* (Lutterworth, 1974)

MacLaine, Shirley, *Dancing in the Light* (Bantam Books, 1985)

— *Out on a Limb* (Bantam Books, 1983)

Luther, Martin, *Works*, 55 vols. (Concordia, 1955–86)

Marshall, Howard, *The Gospel of Luke* (New International Greek Testament Commentary; Paternoster, 1978)

Moltmann, Jürgen, *The Crucified God* (SCM, 1977)

— *A Theology of Hope* (SCM, 1964)

Morris, Leon, *The Apostolic Preaching of the Cross* (IVP, 1972)

— *The Gospel According to John* (Marshall, Morgan and Scott, 1974)

Nehru, Jawaharlal, *The Discovery of India* (Oxford University Press, 1946)

Neill, Stephen, *A History of Christian Missions* (Penguin, 1964)

— *Salvation Today* (Lutterworth, 1976)

— *Salvation Tomorrow* (Lutterworth, 1976)

Newbigin, Lesslie, *A Faith for This One World* (Lucknow Publishing House, 1961)

— *The Open Secret* (SPCK, 1979)

Ohlrich, Charles, *The Suffering God* (Triangle, 1970)

Panikkar, Raimundo, *The Unknown Christ of Hinduism* (Asian Trading Corporation, 1982)

Pannenberg, Wolfhart, *Basic Questions in Theology*, vol. 1 (SCM, 1967), vol. 2 (SCM, 1971)

— *Jesus: God and Man* (SCM, 1976)

— *Theology and the Kingdom of God* (Westminster, 1975)

Pannenberg, Wolfhart, *et al.*, *Revelation as History* (Macmillan, 1969)

Potter, Philip, *Life in All Its Fulness* (World Council of Churches, 1978)

— *Your Kingdom Come* (World Council of Churches, 1980)

Ridderbos, Hermann, *The Coming of the Kingdom* (Presbyterian and Reformed, 1962)

Schaeffer, Francis A., *Pollution and the Death of Man* (Hodder and Stoughton, 1970)

Senior, Donald, and Stuhlmueller, Carrol, *The Biblical Foundations for Missions* (SCM,1983)

Song, Choan-Seng, *Christian Mission in Reconstruction* (Christian Literature Society, 1975)

Smeaton, George, *The Doctrine of the Holy Spirit* (Banner of Truth, 1982)

Snaith, N. H., *Distinctive Ideas of the Old Testament* (Epworth Press, 1944)

Sumithra, Sunand, *Revolution as Revelation* (doctoral dissertation for Tübingen University) (International Christian Network and Theological Research and Communication Institute, New Delhi, 1984)

Taylor, John V., *The Go-between God* (SCM, 1979)

Winter, Ralph D., and Hawthorne, Steven C. (eds.), *Perspectives on the World Christian Movement: A Reader* (William Carey Library, 1981)

The World Mission of the Church: Findings and Recommendations of the Meeting of The International Missionary Council, Tambaram, 1938 (International Missionary Council, 1938)

Notes

Preface (pp. 11–12)

1 'The Bible and Theology in Asia Today: Declaration of the Sixth Asia Theological Association Theological Consultation', in *The Bible and Theology in Asian Contexts* (Asia Theological Association, 1984), p. 8.

1. From Edinburgh to Bangkok (pp. 15–31)

1 A quotation from James Scherer's essay 'Ecumenical Mandates for Mission', in N. A. Horner (ed.), *Protestant Crosscurrents in Mission* (Abingdon, 1968) pp. 19–49). I am indebted to R. E. Hedlund's *Roots of the Great Debate in Mission* (Evangelical Literature Service, 1981) for his useful compilation of various documents that have been helpful in my study.

2 Hedlund, *op. cit.*, p. 32.

3 Ralph D. Winter and Steven C. Hawthorne (eds.), *Perspectives on the World Christian Movement: A Reader* (William Carey Library, 1981), p. 228.

4 M. K. Kuriakose (ed.), *History of Christianity in India: Source Materials* (Indian Theological Library no. 9; Serampore University), p. 303.

5 Hedlund, *op. cit.*, pp. 306f.

6 *Ibid.*, p. 843.

7 Hedlund, *op. cit.*, p. 186.

8 *Ibid.*, p. 186.

9 *Ibid.*, p. 9.

10 *Ibid.*, p. 40.

11 *Ibid.*

12 John Hick develops this idea in his essay 'The Non-Absoluteness of Christianity' in *The Myth of Christian*

216

Uniqueness; John Hick and Paul Knitter (eds.) (Orbis Books, 1988), pp. 16–36.

13 Hedlund, *op. cit.*

14 *Ibid.*, p. 57.

15 *Ibid.*, p. 59.

16 *Ibid.*

17 Kuriakose, *op. cit.*, p. 344.

18 Jawaharlal Nehru, *The Discovery of India* (Oxford University Press, 1946), p. 337.

19 *Ibid.*

20 *The World Mission of the Church: Findings and Recommendations of the Meeting of the International Missionary Council, Tambaram, 1938* (International Missionary Council, 1938), p. 32.

21 *Ibid.*, p. 33.

22 *Ibid.*

23 *Ibid.*, p. 34.

24 *Ibid.*, p. 41.

25 *Ibid.*, p. 42.

26 *Ibid.*

27 *Ibid.*

28 *Ibid.*, p. 43.

29 *Ibid.*, p. 96.

30 *Ibid.*, p. 73.

31 *Ibid.*, p. 42.

32 *Ibid.*, p. 124.

33 *Ibid.*, p. 126.

34 *Ibid.*

35 *Ibid.*, p. 128.

36 *Ibid.*, p. 180.

37 *The World Mission of the Church*, p. 180.

38 Harvey T. Hoekstra, *The World Council of Churches and the Demise of Evangelism* (Tyndale House, 1979), p. 42. Hoekstra surveys the movement extensively, particularly its relationship to evangelism. He has made abundant use of the original documents, which has been helpful in my own study.

39 *Ibid.*, p. 43.

40 Unpublished Ghana papers, WCC archives; quoted in Hoekstra, *op. cit.*, p. 43.

41 Hoekstra, *op. cit.*, p. 49.

42 Hedlund, *op. cit.*, p. 113.

43 Hoekstra, *op. cit.*, p. 68.

44 *Ibid.*, p. 69.

45 World Council of Churches; *The Church for Others and the Church for the World* (1967), p. 78.

46 *Ibid.*, pp. 16f.

47 Hoekstra, *op. cit.*, pp. 58–59.

48 *Ibid.*, p. 101.

2. Mission or missions? (pp. 32–51)

1 Stephen Neill, *Salvation Tomorrow* (Lutterworth, 1976), p. 57.

2 Lesslie Newbigin, *A Faith for This One World* (Lucknow Publishing House, 1961), pp. 108f.

3 *Ibid.*, p. 109.

5 Neill, *op. cit.*, pp. 28ff. I have utilized Neill's summary with some of my own comments.

6 Raimundo Panikkar, *The Unknown Christ of Hinduism* (Asian Trading Corporation, 1982), p. 31.

7 *Ibid.*, p. 2.

8 *Ibid.*, p. 5.

9 *Ibid.*

10 *Ibid.*, p. 163.

11 *Ibid.*, p. 168.

12 *Ibid.*, p. 169.

13 John Hick and Paul Knitter (eds.) *The Myth of Christian Uniqueness* (Orbis Books, 1988), p. vii.

14 Neill, *op. cit.*, p. 40.

15 Philip Potter, *Life in all its Fulness* (World Council of Churches, 1978), p. 73.

16 *Ibid.*

17 *Ibid.*, p. 74.

18 *Ibid.*

19 *Ibid.*

20 *Ibid.*

21 *Ibid.*

22 *Ibid.*

23 *Ibid.*

24 Harvey T. Hoekstra, *The World Council of Churches and the Demise of Evangelism* (Tyndale House, 1979), p. 70.

25 Quoted from J. Hoekendijke, 'The Church in Missionary Thinking', *International Review of Missions*, 41 (1952), pp. 332f., by Choan-Seng Song, *Christian Mission in Reconstruction* (Christian Literature Society, 1975), p. 62.

26 Hoekstra, *op. cit.*, p. 88.

27 M. M. Thomas, *Towards a Theology of Contemporary Ecumenism* (Christian Literature Service (WCC, 1978), p. 182, quoted in Hoekstra, *op. cit.*, p. 74.

28 *Ibid.*, p. 168.

29 Sunand Sumithra, *Revolution as Revelation* (doctoral dissertation for Tübingen University) (International Christian Network and Theological Research and Communication Institute, New Delhi, 1984), p. 23.

30 Hoekstra, *op. cit.*, p. 169.

3. The Old Testament foundation (pp. 55–79)

1 Hans-Georg Gadamer has made a significant contribution in this area, particularly through his book *Truth and Method* (Sheed and Ward, London, 1975).

2 Ken Gnanakan, 'God in Hinduism', in Bong Rin Ro (ed.), *God in Asian Contexts* (Asia Theological Association, 1984), p. 109.

3 See Francis A. Schaeffer, *Pollution and the Death of Man* (Hodder and Stoughton, 1970). Schaeffer's slim paperback deals convincingly with the Christian attitude to ecological concerns. It also reproduces the devastating attack on western Christianity made by Lynn White Jr in his influential article, 'The Historical Roots of our Ecological Crisis', in *Science*, Vol. 155 (1967), pp. 1203–1207.

4 Edmond Jacob, *The Theology of the Old Testament* (Hodder and Stoughton, 1958), p. 138. Although I have given only a few references to Jacob's book, I have drawn several ideas from it.

5 *Ibid.*, p. 137.

6 Lesslie Newbigin, *The Open Secret* (SPCK, 1978), p. 75.

7 *Ibid.*, p. 76.

8 *Ibid.*, p. 78.

4. God and mission (pp. 80–96)

1 Shirley MacLaine's popular paperbacks *Out on a Limb* (Bantam Books, 1983) and *Dancing in the Light* (Bantam Books, 1985) have been very influential and give some interesting insights into the New Age movement.

2 R. A. Finlayson, art. 'Holiness', in J. D. Douglas (ed.), *The New Bible Dictionary* (IVP, 2nd edn., 1982), p. 487.

3 *Ibid.*, p. 488.

4 R. V. G. Tasker, art. 'Wrath', in Douglas (ed.), *op. cit.*, p. 1263.

5 B. A. Milne, art. 'Sin', in Douglas (ed.), *op. cit.*, p. 1119.

6 Leon Morris deals thoroughly with the arguments of C. H. Dodd and B. F. Westcott in his discussion on propitiation in *The Apostolic Preaching of the Cross* (IVP, 1972) pp. 144–213.

7 *Ibid.*, p. 174.

8 *Ibid.*, p. 177.

9 Keith R. Crim (ed.), *The Interpreter's Dictionary of the Bible* (Abingdon, 1979), vol. 2, p. 427. This is a useful study on the Old Testament view of God.

10 N. H. Snaith, *Distinctive Ideas of the Old Testament* (Epworth Press, 1944), pp. 94ff.

11 Edmond Jacob, *The Theology of the Old Testament* (Hodder and Stoughton, 1958), p. 95.

12 Kazoh Kitamori, *Theology of the Pain of God* (SCM, 1958), pp. 20ff.

13 Dietrich Bonhoeffer, *Letters and Papers from Prison* (SCM, 1971 edition), p. 361, quoted in Jürgen Moltmann, *The Crucified God* (SCM, 1977), p. 47.

14 *Ibid.*, p. 48.

15 Charles Ohlrich, *The Suffering God* (Triangle, 1970), pp. 54ff.

16 *Ibid.*, p. 55.

5. Promise, history and mission (pp. 97–112)

1 Wolfhart Pannenberg's theology is marked by a deep concern for history. I have developed this extensively in my doctoral thesis *God and Man in Universal History* (unpublished, University of London, 1980).

2 Wolfhart Pannenberg *et al.*, *Revelation as History* (Macmillan, 1969), p. 50.

3 Wolfhart Pannenberg, *Jesus: God and Man* (SCM, 1976), p. 69.

4 *Ibid.*

5 *Ibid.*

6 *Ibid.*

7 Wolfhart Pannenberg, *Basic Questions in Theology*, vol. 1 (SCM, 1967), p. 18.

8 *Ibid.*, p. 18.

9 'The Beginnings of Christian Theology', in Ernst Käseman, *New Testament Questions of Today* (SCM, 1969), pp. 82–107.

10 Alan Cole, *Exodus* (Tyndale Old Testament Commentaries: IVP, 1973), p. 24.

11 See Keith R. Crim (ed.), *The Interpreter's Dictionary of the Bible* (Abingdon, 1979), vol. 2, pp. 409ff.

12 *E.g.*, Is. 2:12–21; Ezk. 13:5; Joel 1:15; 2:1, 11; Zp. 1:7–18; Zc. 14:1.

13 F. F. Bruce, *The Time is Fulfilled* (Eerdmans, 1978), p. 61.

14 Jürgen Moltmann, *A Theology of Hope* (SCM, 1964), p. 147.

15 *Ibid.*

6. The kingdom horizon (pp. 113–135)

1 Lesslie Newbigin, *The Open Secret* (SPCK, 1979), p. 32.

2 *Ibid.*, p. 33.

3 In this section I summarize the useful discussion on the use of *basileia* in the NT in B. Klappert, 'King, Kingdom', in Colin Brown (ed.), *The New International Dictionary of the New Testament*, vol. 2 (Paternoster, 1971), pp. 381ff.

4 Howard Marshall, *The Gospel of Luke* (The New International Greek Testament Commentary; Paternoster, 1978), p. 655.

5 Some important writings of Pannenberg's on this theme are *Basic Questions in Theology*, vol. 1 (SCM, 1970), vol. 2 (SCM, 1971); and Richard John Neuhaus (ed.), *Theology and the Kingdom of God* (Westminster, 1975).

6 G. E. Ladd, *A Theology of the New Testament* (Lutterworth, 1974), p. 91. Ladd's insights have been very useful in my study.

7 Hermann Ridderbos, *The Coming of the Kingdom* (Presbyterian and Reformed, 1962), p. 427. Ridderbos' detailed study has been very helpful in this chapter.

8 Ladd, *op. cit.*, p. 91.

9 See Wolfhart Pannenberg's essay 'Appearance as the Arrival of the Future', in *Theology and the Kingdom of God*, pp. 127–143.

10 *E.g.* Ex. 6:7; 19:5; Lv. 26:12; Je. 30:22; Ezk. 36:28.

Paul's universal perspective (pp. 136–153)

1 Donald Senior and Carrol Stuhlmueller, *The Biblical Foundations for Missions* (SCM, 1983), p. 261.

2 *Ibid.*, p. 261.

3 F. F. Bruce, *The Acts of the Apostles* (Tyndale Press, 1952), p. 31.

4 *Ibid.*

5 Senior and Stuhlmueller, *op. cit.*, p. 193.

6 *Ibid.*, p. 191.

7 *Ibid.*, p. 196ff. Senior and Stuhlmueller develop these themes more fully, and I have drawn out only some of their points for our discussion.

8 Senior and Stuhlmueller draw their inspiration from, and quote from, Eduard Schweizer, 'The Church as the Missionary Body of Christ', in his collection of essays, *Neotestamentica* (Zwingli Verlag, 1963), p. 325.

9 I have developed some of these aspects in an article published in Bong Rin Ro (ed.), *God in Asian Contexts* (Asia Theological Association, 1988), pp. 108ff.

10 Senior and Stuhlmueller, *op. cit.*, p. 197.

11 William Barclay, *Letters to Philippians, Colossians and Thessalonians* (Saint Andrew Press, 1972), p. 144.

12 *Ibid.*, p. 148.

13 *Ibid.*

14 See art. 'Wisdom' by H. Weigelt, in *The New International Dictionary of New Testament Theology*, vol. 3, p. 1030.

8. The missiology of John (pp. 154–173)

1 Leon Morris, *The Gospel According to John* (Marshall, Morgan and Scott, 1974), p. 80.

2 Bong Rin Ro (ed.), *God in Asian Contexts* (Asia Theological Association, 1988).

3 Morris, *op. cit.*, p. 81.

4 Morris, *op. cit.*, p. 126.

5 *Ibid.*

6 Jn. 7:7; 8:23; 12:31; 14:30; 15:18; 17:9; 14 – 16; 1 Jn. 2:15.

7 H. Ridderbos, *The Coming of the Kingdom* (Presbyterian and Reformed, 1962), p. 62.

8 Gustavo Gutiérrez, *A Theology of Liberation* (SCM, 1977), p. 152.

9 *Ibid.*, p. 167.

10 Choan-Seng Song, *Christian Mission in Reconstruction* (Christian Literature Society, 1975), p. 54.

11 *Ibid.*

12 *Ibid.*, p. 52.

13 *Ibid.*, p. 56.

14 *Ibid.*, p. 57.

15 *Ibid.*

16 *Ibid.*, p. 59.
17 *Ibid.*, p. 54.
18 *Ibid.*

9. The role of the Holy Spirit (pp. 174–194)

1 Roland Allen, *The Ministry of the Spirit* (selected writings, ed. David M. Paton; World Dominion Press, 1960) p. 20.
2 John V. Taylor, *The Go-between God* (SCM, 1979), p. 3.
3 Allen, *op. cit.*, p. 3.
4 *Ibid.*
5 *Ibid.*
6 Harry R. Boer developed his thesis on the Holy Spirit and mission for his doctoral dissertation written for the Department of Missions of the Free University of Amsterdam. The book is published as *Pentecost and Mission* (Eerdmans, 1961).
7 Allen, *op. cit.*, p. 17.
8 *Ibid.*, p. 21.
9 *Ibid.*, p. 8.
10 *Ibid.*
11 Acts 2:16–17, 21, 39; 3:25, 26; 4:18.
12 Boer, *op. cit.*, p. 47.
13 *Ibid.*, p. 66.
14 *Ibid.*, p. 74.
15 *Ibid.*, p. 95.
16 *Ibid.*, p. 129.
17 Allen, *op. cit.*, p. 17.
18 This we have already considered in our discussion on the kingdom of God.
19 Taylor, *op. cit.*, p. 134.
20 *Ibid.*, p. 259.
21 George Smeaton, *The Doctrine of the Holy Spirit* (Banner of Truth, 1982), p. 259.
22 *Ibid.*, p. 260.
23 *Ibid.*, pp. 260f.

10. The church and God's mission today (pp. 197–212)

1 John Calvin, *Institutes of the Christian Religion* (1536; MacDonald Publishing Co., no date) IV. 1.9., p. 545.

2 Quoted by Paul D. L. Avis, *The Church in the Theology of the Reformers* (John Knox, 1981), p. 17.

3 Cardinal Robert Bellarmine (1524–1621), quoted in Stephen Neill, *A History of Christian Missions* (Penguin, 1964), p. 221.

4 Quoted in Avis, *op. cit.*, p. 173, from Luther, *Works*, 55 vols. (Concordia, 1955–1986), vol. 39, p. 319.

5 Philip Potter, 'From Edinburgh to Melbourne', in the WCC Report, *Your Kingdom Come* (World Council of Churches, 1980), pp. 6–21.

6 John Hick and Paul Knitter (eds.), *The Myth of Christian Uniqueness* (Orbis Books, 1988). I develop my arguments in relation to Hick's and Knitter's concern for a pluralistic theology in detail in my book *The Pluralistic Predicament* (Theological Book Trust, Bangalore, 1992).

7 *Ibid.*, p. vii.

8 *Ibid.*, p. ix.

9 See the essays 'The Cross and the Rainbow' by Stanley J. Samartha (*ibid.*, pp. 69–88) and 'The Jordan, the Tiber and the Ganges' by Raimundo Panikkar (*ibid.*, pp. 89–116).

10 Stephen Neill, *Salvation Tomorrow* (Lutterworth, 1976), p. 148.

11 J. H. Bavinck, *An Introduction to the Science of Missions* (Presbyterian and Reformed, 1960), pp. 271f.

12 Peter Cotterell, *The Eleventh Commandment* (IVP, 1981), p. 17.

13 I myself had earlier argued for *mission* to be seen purely as evangelistic in its intention, and all else to be seen as *ministry*, in my article in AIM Magazine (Evangelical Fellowship of India, March, 1981).